Vimalakirti & the Awakened Heart
A Commentary on *The Sutra that Vimalakirti Speaks*

Vimalakirti & the Awakened Heart
A Commentary on *The Sutra that Vimalakirti Speaks*

Joan Sutherland

Vimalakirti & the Awakened Heart
A Commentary on *The Sutra that Vimalakirti Speaks*
© 2016 Cloud Dragon : The Joan Sutherland Dharma Works
ISBN 978-0-9913569-3-5
Cover design by Laura Star
Printed and bound in the USA

Following Wind Press
Cloud Dragon Dharma Works
Post Office Box 2368
Santa Fe, NM 87504

joansutherlanddharmaworks.org

This is the first volume in a collection called Pilgrim's Bundle, small handbooks for clouds-and-water wanderers on the Way (whether you ever leave home or not), meant to be tucked into a backpack or under a pillow, used, argued with, scribbled on, and shared. The handbooks go deep into tradition and wide into our lives, discussing philosophy, practice, and poetry in a conversational voice and offering a variety of maps, phrasebooks, and never-expiring visas for roaming the Way.

Four English translations of *The Sutra that Vimalakirti Speaks* are widely available, either in book form or on the Internet :

- The clearest and most accessible is Burton Watson's *Vimalakirti Sutra*

- A scholarly version is the second half of a double volume, *The Sutra of Queen Srimala of the Lion's Roar* by Diana Y. Paul and *The Vimalakirti Sutra* by John R. McRae

- In an earlier generation, the Chinese version of the sutra was also translated by the venerable Charles Luk as *The Vimalakirti Nirdesa Sutra*

- The Tibetan version of the sutra, which is somewhat different, is represented by Robert A.F. Thurman's *Vimalakirti Nirdesa Sutra*

In this commentary, the quotations from the sutra are my own versions, based on and much indebted to these translations.

Contents

Preface

There's a myth tucked under layers of philosophical discourse and elaborate description in *The Sutra that Vimalakirti Speaks*. Like all myths, it's a story that speaks to our souls, telling us something timeless about how to navigate the dream of life. The Vimalakirti myth is about developing a peaceful and generous heart in a world of sorrows, and about how the awakening of each of us is an inextricable part of the awakening of the world.

The sutra is written in classical Buddhist style — philosophical discourse, elaborate description — but the myth embedded in it is direct ancestor to the vivid storytelling of Chan and the koans. Koan people, like the descendants in many creative traditions, have the interesting idea that the best way to honor their ancestors is to get busy reworking the inheritance they've received from them. So this commentary engages with the sutra's mythic through-line and the philosophy and practice that seem to reflect it most closely, while leaving the rest to rest in peace.

The commentary began as a series of talks in Santa Fe, New Mexico in the spring and summer of 2011. The talks were transcribed and edited by Sarah Bender, Sensei and others, and then I extensively revised and expanded the transcript in 2016. I'm aware that this kind of ramble through an ancient text asks something of contemporary readers ... and I believe the effort is more than worth it, since the ancestors have an awful lot to tell us. So I'll give it to you like this, close to the old bone, and if you make poetry out of it or set it to a modern beat, that's just as it should be, too.

"May it give you as much joy to eat as it gave me to make."

by the summer sea, 2016

Vimalakirti's Gate

Introduction

The Sutra that Vimalakirti Speaks[1] is a two-thousand-year-old Buddhist text that tells a strange and wonderful story. At the center of the story is a man named Vimalakirti, who is lying on a sickbed in an otherwise empty room in an otherwise empty house in a city in northern India. He's considered a bodhisattva, which is to say an awakened person who has chosen not to melt into nirvana, so that he can remain in the world to work for the awakening of everyone else.

The sutra is also called *The Reconciliation of Dualities*, and the first apparent duality has just appeared : how is it that a deeply enlightened person is sick? Isn't the whole point of enlightenment to elevate someone beyond the limitations and sorrows of ordinary life? But Vimalakirti doesn't seem to want to be elevated. He says, "I am sick because the whole world is sick."

1　A sutra is a canonical Buddhist text; the Chinese translated this Sanskrit word with their word for 'warp,' as in weaving on a loom

The implications of this explanation, which is also an expression of love and a vow, reverberate through the text.

The sutra was written down in India about five hundred years after the time of Shakyamuni Buddha. The Buddha taught during the middle of the first millennium BCE, when a revulsion against the excesses of the Iron Age was being expressed not just in Northern India, but by figures like Socrates in Greece, the early Daoists in China, and countless women and men whose names we don't remember. They expressed a collective anguish about the violence and brutality of the time. Many of the antidotes they offered involved withdrawal from the fray, intense self-examination, and meditative practices. Nothing else can happen, they believed, until the fever breaks — and if the culture won't calm down, they could at least treat themselves, one by one. (In fact, the word nirvana is etymologically linked to a word that means the cool after a fever.)[2]

The Sutra that Vimalakirti Speaks comes from a time of powerful tension within Buddhism between this classical vision, with its focus on attaining freedom from being reborn into a suffering world, and the emerging Mahayana, with its commitment to staying in the world to help all beings attain freedom from suffering. The fever had cooled enough that people were starting to formulate the antidote to the antidote, as it were : when not consumed by delirium, when not focused on escaping the delirium of others, we begin to turn back toward the world. Hearts shuttered in fear yearn to open again to something larger than self-preservation, and the sutra offered a

---

2 This is a quick and dirty version of an idea formulated by the philosopher Karl Popper, which was taken up by the scholar of religions Karen Armstrong in her book *The Great Transformation*

perspective and a practice to support those who wanted to turn back to the world. But it couldn't completely shed the habit of turning away — so much so that it ends with a passage about practicing really hard so you can be reborn in a better place, reversing the core message of the text.

The thread we're following through the sutra is an early version of what we'd call endarkenment now, though the sutra never uses that word. In broad strokes, enlightenment is about the brilliant illumination that lifts us out of the suffering world and is the focus of classical Buddhist literature; endarkenment is about the radiance of the deeps that lets us find home *in* the world. Endarkenment is the heart that breaks open to life, rests comfortably on the unfathomable mystery of existence, and is easy with uncertainty, complexity, and what courses underground. Enlightenment and endarkenment are both essential to awakening, and Vimalakirti was one of the earliest voices for including the dark, an inclusion that makes awakening whole.[3]

When the sutra arrived in China, it must have seemed wonderfully familiar to the early Buddhists there, who were steeped in their native Daoism. Daoism puts the origin of everything in the Great Mysterious, the primordial darkness out of which the lights of the visible world stream. The sutra offered the *Yin* to complement enlightenment's *Yang* and became an important influence on the Chan and koan traditions,[4]

---

3 In this commentary I make a distinction between enlightenment and awakening that isn't always explicit in the text : enlightenment refers to the illuminating insight that is part of awakening, and awakening is a lifelong process that also includes endarkenment; see the section "Mind and Heart" for more

4 Chan is one of the schools of Chinese Buddhism and the origin of the koan tradition; Chan is the Chinese pronunciation of the word later pronounced Zen in Japanese

which took Vimalakirti as one of their ancestors.

My commentary follows Chan and the koans in focusing on the parts of the sutra that most clearly lay out the brief for staying in the heartbreaking world. Still, let's acknowledge that the struggle between yearning for relief and yearning to be helpful doesn't just play itself out at a philosophical level; it's in many of us, every day. The liberating message of this sutra is that the two aren't mutually exclusive : choose your life, and keep choosing your life day by day ... and find peace *there*. Vimalakirti lays out a challenging and extraordinarily beautiful way of doing that.

The sutra was also popular in China because it's about a householder, living the kind of life many people could relate to. Vimalakirti embodies a number of provocative dualities in addition to being a sick bodhisattva : he's a rich man who gives all his money to the poor, someone who lives among family and employees on a great estate but remains solitary, has children and frequents brothels but is celibate, goes to the bars but doesn't get drunk. He's equally at home in a court of law, the women's quarters, a classroom, or standing on a street corner. The necessary antidote to any situation, he teaches humility to brahmins[5] and helps ordinary people gain prosperity and political power. The koans speak of him as an extraordinary improbability.

In the koan tradition, when we're presented with an apparent duality, we resolve it not by choosing *A* or *B* but by looking for *C*, that unexpected thing that can embrace both

---

5   Brahmins are the religious ceremonialists and teachers responsible for the vast array of Hindu rituals, and therefore for the continued good order of the cosmos

A and *B* and create something new from them. In this sutra, Vimalakirti himself is *C*, the reconciliation of the opposites. In the koan tradition he was known as Pure Name, and the Chan teacher Huangbo says that this represents the coming together of the vastness (pure), and a particular embodied being (name).[6] Everything has a name, and everything is vast. That which is nameless and unborn and that which is named and born come together in the person of Vimalakirti, which is to say in each of us.

Vimalakirti speaks to us from within this deepest of all reconciliations, laying out a Way for healing the human heart. The healing takes place in his ten-by-ten-foot room, which is both the space of awakening already present within each of us, and the field of awakening we make together. Step right into the dream of awakening, he's saying. Welcome to your own heart.

---

6 I use 'vastness' rather than 'emptiness' because it's empty only in a technical sense (empty of self-nature); it's actually full to bursting with every-thing that is and might be. This is *shunyata* (which means both empty and pregnant), Dao, plenum, *dharmakaya*, etc. Words like particular, embodied, and material refer to what is often called the world of form, a term that might feel a little distanced from the richness that makes up that world. They're different aspects of the same thing : everything that is.

The Pure Land

This very place is paradise,
this very body, the Buddha
Hakuin

The Sutra that Vimalakirti Speaks begins just outside
Vimalakirti's city, in a beautiful park which a famous courtesan
called Amrapali has loaned to Shakyamuni Buddha. (And giv-
en the conventional morality of the day about courtesans and
holy men, here's our opening duality.) Whenever the Buddha
stops somewhere awhile, a vast assembly of beings gathers to
hear him speak — not just monks, nuns, and laypeople, but
gods, bodhisattvas, heavenly musicians, dragons, phoenixes,
and snake princesses. The sutra begins and ends in this lovely,
fragrant garden.

As is his custom, the Buddha takes questions from the
assembly, and one of his main disciples, Shariputra, steps
forward. Shariputra is so respected for his wisdom that he's
the person to whom Guanyin addresses the *Heart Sutra* :
"Shariputra, form is no other than emptiness, emptiness no
other than form." In *The Vimalakirti Sutra* he's the sincere voice

of ordinary life, with its grounded concerns and familiar ways of seeing things, and his questions keep the majestic narrative rolling. Here at the beginning he asks the question that haunts so many seekers and pilgrims : "You say that this world, this existence of ours, is the Pure Land.[7] But I don't experience it that way; I experience it as full of pain, suffering, horror, and ugliness." In response, the Buddha gets down from his seat and digs his toes into the ground. As soon as he does, the world fills with precious jewels, and Shariputra sees it as the Pure Land.

When the Buddha literally comes down to earth and digs his toes in, he doesn't instantly *transform* the world into the Pure Land. Instead, Shariputra says that now he *sees* the world as the Pure Land. The nature of the world hasn't changed, but Shariputra's ability to experience it has. "When my mind doesn't arise, all things are blameless," as the koan says.[8] This complicated, nuanced, gorgeous, difficult, confusing world *as it is* is already the Pure Land, and now Shariputra sees that that was always true.

The Sutra That Vimalakirti Speaks lays out a couple of big questions right at the beginning : What does it mean that this world as it is is the Pure Land? And what is the shift in perception that enables Shariputra to know that?

Then, through either omniscience or rumor, depending on your viewpoint, the Buddha knows that Vimalakirti is nearby, and that he's sick. The Buddha wants to send a personal

---

7   The Pure Land, Sukhavati in Sanskrit, is a kind of heavenly paradise where some Buddhists throughout the ages have believed that you can be reborn after death, if you do certain devotional practices in this life. For example, Japanese Pure Land Buddhists constantly repeat the Nembutsu, *Namu Amida Butsu*, Homage to Amitabha Buddha (the Buddha of Infinite Light).

8   The koan borrows from Sengcan's poem *Trust in Mind (Xinxinming)*

representative to offer his respects and condolences to Vimalakirti. It's probably not an accident that the Buddha's thoughts turn to the sick bodhisattva so close on the heels of his dialogue with Shariputra. Perhaps he wants his disciples to experience a way of being brokenhearted different from the one Shariputra expresses — one that turns toward the world rather than away from it, and opens the heart to awakening.

The Buddha asks, one by one, his five hundred great disciples and all of the bodhisattvas to go, but they decline. They say that they've tangled with Vimalakirti in the past and don't want to be alone in a room with him because he's too disturbing. Their reluctance is understandable, because Vimalakirti confronts us with a way of being that is awesome (in the true sense of the word), in both what it promises and what it demands. It *is* an extraordinary improbability, like the vows we take in a refuge ceremony[9] — an impossible aspiration that we are likely never to succeed at. But if the demand is large, so is the promise : every human heart healed, beginning the healing of the world.

Finally Manjushri, the bodhisattva of insight, agrees to visit Vimalakirti, and everyone decides that a debate between the archetypal bodhisattva of insight and the human bodhisattva of great compassion is something not to be missed. So Manjushri sets off for Vimalakirti's place, trailed by 32,000 beings who want to see this conversation happen — even if they're not quite ready to *have* the conversation themselves.

---

9 Our tradition includes the Ceremony of Taking Refuge in the Bodhisattva Way, during which we take sixteen vows, including three professions of refuge in awakening, the Way, and our companions, and thirteen impossible promises about doing good and refraining from doing harm

At Vimalakirti's

Did you come for the Way or did you come for a seat?

Vimalakirti

Meanwhile, Vimalakirti — again by rumor or omniscience, depending — knows they're coming. So he empties his whole estate, ordering every stick of furniture and every piece of art removed, and he asks everybody in the household to leave for the day. When Manjushri and his retinue reach Vimalakirti's house, the only thing they see is the bodhisattva lying on his sickbed in a ten-by-ten-foot room.

If the Buddha's voluptuous garden with its vast assembly and Vimalakirti's solitary, empty room are polar opposites, there does seem to be a psychic link between the Buddha and Vimalakirti, and each is keenly aware of the other. There's a parallel with the koan known as "The True Qian," based on a folktale about a woman who is simultaneously living an eventful life and home in bed, delirious with illness.[10] In the

---

10   The full koan can be found in *Acequias & Gates : Miscellaneous Koans and Miscellaneous Writings on Koans*

end the two Qians reconcile and become one. The koan question is, "Which is the true Qian?" In this sutra, what happens to the 32,000 — which is to say, all of us — when we reconcile for ourselves the park and the sickroom, the Buddha and Vimalakirti, as well as their doubles, Manjushri and the Goddess?

Manjushri and his retinue, processing from the Buddha to Vimalakirti, form a sort of living bridge between them — set in motion by the Buddha, welcomed by Vimalakirti. It might be important that the members of the retinue are at first reluctant to bridge that particular gap, content to remain in the garden (Sunday in the park with Buddha!) with their fixed ideas of purity, defilement, and right practice, safe from the subversions of uncomfortable questions.

Vimalakirti wastes no time, confronting them with the stark fact of himself, all distractions removed. A sick bodhisattva? Isn't the whole point of dedicating yourself to becoming a bodhisattva so that you don't have to be sick anymore? Perhaps the assembly was hoping that the sword of Manjushri's bright knowing would cut through the complexities of Vimalakirti's relentless presentation of life as it is. In the end, they find that healing is something quite different, and the path to it leads through Vimalakirti's gate.

And now it's time for Shariputra to ask another question. He looks around and says, "But, sir, the room is completely empty. There are no chairs for anyone to sit on." The fact that 32,000 beings have managed to fit comfortably into Vimalakirti's ten-by-ten-foot room doesn't seem to have made much of an impression, but the issue of where everyone might sit has Shariputra worried.

Vimalakirti responds, "Let me ask you, did you come for the Way[11] or are you looking for a place to sit?" That's something

---

11 'Way' is a translation of 'Dharma,' which means both the Buddhist teachings and the way the universe is, much like the Dao (Tao) in Chinese

we can ask ourselves. Which did we come for, and what are those seats? Do we come for happiness, wisdom, peace, escape, meaning, greater compassion, relief of suffering? Or do we come willing to follow the Way wherever it leads us, even into this dodgy sickroom with its sudden portals to other worlds?

Vimalakirti says that you have to give up everything in order to seek the Way, including the bedrock orthodoxies of Buddhism. He runs through a whole list of those, beginning at the beginning with the Four Noble Truths : if you're looking at unsatisfactoriness, its causes, its end, and the path to that end, what you're actually seeking is not the Way but unsatisfactoriness, its causes, its end, and the path to that end.[12] The same is true for nirvana; the Three Treasures of Buddha, Dharma, and Sangha;[13] and all other formulations and theories, however central to Buddhist doctrine. The Way is none of the techniques and practices taught over the last two thousand five hundred years, and by other people for thousands of years before that; the Way isn't meditation, or inquiry, or even koans. It's neither what you think you're looking for nor the techniques you think will help you find it. In all these instances you're putting something else in place of the wild and undomesticated Dao. Vimalakirti says that you have to be willing to give up your body and your life, let alone a seat, for the Way.

If the Way is something other than the teachings *about* the Way, you can let fall away all the things you think the Way is,

---

12   The Four Noble Truths, considered the foundations of classical Buddhism, are usually translated as : 1. Life is suffering. 2. There is a cause of suffering. 3. There is cessation of suffering. 4. There is a way to the cessation of suffering. *Dukkha*, the Sanskrit word usually translated as 'suffering,' is perhaps more helpfully thought of as 'unsatisfactoriness' or 'incompleteness.'

13   Buddha, teachings, and community; or awakening, the Way and our companions

or want it to be, or have been led to expect it is. You accept the condition of seatlessness and stand on the bare ground. When you do that, what walks toward you? That's the Way : that mystery which cannot be expressed or explained or anticipated, which until the moment it appears is by its nature unimaginable to you. The Way is the willingness to seek that, and nothing short of that.

But Vimalakirti is also a householder sensitive to the needs of his guests, and so he contacts a buddha in another realm and orders 32,000 large lion thrones for the use and comfort of his visitors. Now everyone has a place to sit. (To this day, the room that a Chan or Zen teacher uses is ten feet by ten feet, in honor of Vimalakirti's room and what can happen there. So work in the room takes place in Vimalakirti's hundred square feet, on 32,000 lion thrones, everyone welcome.)

The sutra remarks that, despite the tens of thousands of visitors on their individual thrones, Vimalakirti's house isn't deformed by this, nor is the block on which the house sits, nor is the city. There's no cartoon image of the exterior of the house, rocking on its foundations, bulging with bodhisattvas. This seems like a small but telling detail, indicating that this isn't a practice about display or having lots of precious things we do and special ways we do them. We are the modest room that can contain 32,000 lion thrones, and anybody walking by on the street wouldn't know. Each of us, in our ordinary householder's life, is that room, with all its beauty, richness, despair, difficulty, tragedy, and triumph going on inside.

Not Two

When asked about the essence of Zen, Suzuki Shunryu said
that he could sum it up in two words : not always so.

Nonduality, one of the great themes of *The Sutra that
Vimalakirti Speaks*, is called by the Chinese, with typical
pungency, 'not two.' Vimalakirti lives the life of a householder
and is deeply committed to his spiritual practice, without
seeing them as separate, let alone mutually exclusive. When
the Buddha tries to recruit an emissary to Vimalakirti, the
candidates recount their previous encounters with him, and we
learn that Vimalakirti spoke often of this particular not-two.
Don't be so literal, he counsels; leaving the household life isn't
about renouncing your family and putting on robes; it's about
leaving harmful views and bad habits and putting on practices
like meditation, which you can do anywhere.

The same goes for what you consider your place of practice; it's not a physical location but your own heart-mind, your
resolve and curiosity and aspiration, your generosity, vows,
and forbearance — not to mention the intricate web of causes
and conditions, earthly desires, and everything that lives. We

make the temple or mountain hermitage or ancient shrine for our practice out of the stuff and matter of our daily lives, out of our moments in the sunlight and under the stars. Even quiet sitting has nothing to do with sitting quietly; true quiet sitting is being in deep meditation while going about what Vimalakirti calls the ceremonies of daily life, having a heart-mind fixed neither on externals nor on internal states. He doesn't elaborate, but it's natural to wonder what that third state of heart-mind, including both inner and outer awareness but defined by neither, might be.

As we in this koan tradition are making community, we've looked for our ancestors : who are the people who asked the same kinds of questions we ask, and came up with ways to embody not-two that feel congruent and harmonious with our own lives? One group of ancestors that has come alive for some of us is the Daoren, women who lived about a thousand years after this sutra came to China. Daoren means People of the Way. They were the Vimalakirtis of their time, women who chose not to enter the monastic institutions of Buddhism like the convents, but also not to live the lives that were otherwise awaiting them in society. They came together in autonomous intentional communities and lived by customs of spiritual discipline that they developed and agreed upon together. Because of the integrity of the way they lived, they were trusted even though they were outside the culture's usual structures of authority. They were able to spend time with women of different walks of life, from farming women in the fields to women cloistered in upper-class and literati families.

In the Daoren tradition as I understand it, the practice of not-two is embodied in subverting and connecting. By crossing the barriers set up around the lives of women in different classes, they subverted women's segregation and connected them with one other. Gossip, news, and messages were passed from street to inner chamber and back again, medicines from the woods dispensed in bedrooms, ideas debated and resources shared.

At a practical level, *The Vimalakirti Sutra* hopes to subvert any compartmentalization in our lives, especially with regard to the daily and the spiritual; it reconnects us with any aspect of life we might think we have to renounce. Philosophically, Vimalakirti is subverting anything that reinforces our tendency to make two, to divide things up into this pile and that pile, us and them, black and white, right and wrong. Dualism is a trick of the mind, not a description of the way the world actually is. If we can subvert the habits of mind that make dualities, we can take the next step, which is to begin to connect those things that have been separated by that trick.

Clear out the bramble thicket of twos, divisions, categories, and separations, and then connect what has been artificially sundered; bring things back together. That applies not only to our relationships with each other — the apparently infinite ability of human beings to find different categories of *us* and *them* — but also between us and the other creatures of the world, between us and the natural world as a whole.

When we take up the subverting and connecting that *The Sutra That Vimalakirti Speaks* and the Daoren share, we are becoming more realistic. We are coming closer to the way things actually are, because the world as it actually is, when the dualistic trick of the mind is not operating, is thunderously and radiantly not two.

Bodhisattvas of the Tilty World

Because we are born and we die, there is illness.
Vimalakirti

When Vimalakirti begins to speak from his sickbed,
it's with absolute, unquestioned, unmitigated, unbuffered,
uncompromised allegiance to this world — and his illness is
part of what he has allegiance to. For the purposes of this story
Vimalakirti's is a physical illness, but it could as easily be any
kind of dis-ease, any way we're off-balance, internally or in our
relationships with the world, or the world's relationship with
us. When Vimalakirti talks about illness, he's talking about
whatever's tilty in our lives, and he's saying that that quality of
tiltiness is fundamental to this world. If our world is already
a Pure Land, it's the tilty Pure Land, where we're constantly
being rocked and never quite find center, or find it only for a
moment before we get knocked off balance again.

Later in the story Vimalakirti makes contact with a beautiful non-tilty world called Many Fragrances. Its inhabitants
build their halls and towers out of fragrances, stroll the scented

ground, and cultivate sweet-smelling gardens. The aroma of
their food wafts to countless worlds in all directions. When
Vimalakirti opens up some kind of wormhole to Many Fragrances, the inhabitants look at our world and exclaim that it
looks pretty tough here. Our world is called Saha, Endurance;
there's general agreement with Shariputra's assessment of life
here as a lot of suffering that has to be borne.

But the inexorable Vimalakirti advises everyone not to
rank : that's the World of Many Fragrances, this is the Tilty
World. We should understand that the universe has infinite
possibilities, and if we're here our job is to accept the offer
of this world, not just to yearn for rebirth in some other one.
In many ways the sutra is about transforming our attitude
towards our own lives from endurance to active acceptance,
even welcome.

Part of taking up the way of not-two is accepting the offer
this world makes to us, which is to be an unbalanced being
in an unbalanced world. If the negative qualities of the offer
are obvious, there's also a positive quality, which is a kind of
creativity. We don't just look at the instability of the world
as the cause of suffering and complication; we can also see it
as a source of creative responses to those very difficulties. In
fact, Vimalakirti says, ten good practices have arisen here in
the Tilty World and nowhere else : for example, generosity
in response to poverty, forbearance in response to anger, and
meditation in response to distractedness. Also four ways of
attracting people to the Way : charity, kind words, working
for the good of others, and sharing in the hardships of others.
These are the gifts of our *saha* world.

Not-two expresses the oneness of all things, and it also

implies their multiplicity. You can deal with the trick of the mind that is duality by applying the sword that cuts into one, and you can deal with it by noticing the infinite proliferation of beings and viewpoints and possibilities that make up the universe, so that only-two suddenly seems like an impoverished alternative. Vimalakirti implies that we bodhisattvas-in-training should avoid thinking of the bodhisattva as a template of perfection we're going to squeeze ourselves into; in an off-balance world that invites our flexibility and improvisation, there are a lot of different ways to be a bodhisattva, and the sutra names many of them.

I used to think that this was just part of the tendency in the old texts to elaborate : the chiliocosms upon chiliocosms,[14] and all the wonderful jewels, flowers, music. But now I think this is actually a deep Dharma point : there isn't *a* bodhisattva; there are Unblinking Bodhisattva, Wonderful Arm Bodhisattva, Jewel Hand Bodhisattva, Lion Mind Bodhisattva, Pure Emancipation Bodhisattva, Universal Maintenance Bodhisattva, Jewel Courage Bodhisattva, Roots of Joy Bodhisattva, Joyful Vision Bodhisattva, Sounds of Thunder Bodhisattva, Serene Capacity Bodhisattva, Store of Virtue Bodhisattva, Delights in the Real Bodhisattva. And then there are three that clearly show the absence of a single template for our spiritual lives : Viewing Equality Bodhisattva, Viewing Inequality Bodhisattva, and Viewing Equality and Inequality Bodhisattva.

This is just a fraction of the titles in the sutra, and the invitation is to discover your particular expression of bodhisattvaness. In the Tilty World, you figure out whether you're Jeweled Hand Bodhisattva or Roots of Joy Bodhisattva,

---

14   In Buddhist cosmology, a chiliocosm is a collection of 1,000 x 1,000 world-systems; I just enjoy the word

understanding that you might be different bodhisattvas at
different times in your life — and maybe more often than not
feeling a bit humble about it all : Fingers Crossed Bodhisattva,
Pretty Close Bodhisattva, Not a Bad Morning Bodhisattva,
Flying by the Seat of My Pants Bodhisattva.

Someone suggested that Shariputra acts as the Universal
Maintenance Bodhisattva in this sutra, the great celestial
janitor, whose subversions of high seriousness keep the story
connected to the actual concerns of the human heart — and
sometimes the human bottom and the human tummy.

One of the profound beauties of the Mahayana vision is
a sense that we human bodhisattvas aren't doing this alone;
everything in the world is engaged in the work of awakening,
everything is its own kind of bodhisattva : Cow Bodhisattva,
Fool's Gold Bodhisattva, Scuffed Slipper Bodhisattva. (Do
you imagine the right slipper and the left each has its own
bodhisattva path?) At the end of the sutra Shakyamuni calls
this infinite collaborative effort the work of the buddhas. In
some worlds radiant light does the work, in others it might be
gardens, groves, towers, clothing, food, the body, empty space,
dreams, metaphors, words, silence, even the 84,000 earthly
desires — in other words, pretty much anything. So we particularly human expressions of bodhisattvaness have all these
comrades to help us with our impossible promise to the world.

Vimalakirti & Manjushri I

Mind & Heart

Then the brightness wanes,
and the darkness comes with love.
Japanese folk song

Once everyone is comfortably seated, the archetypal dialogue between Vimalakirti and Manjushri begins. Manjushri
is the bodhisattva of *prajna*, which is most often translated as
wisdom, but it might better be thought of as a kind of clear,
bright insight. Wisdom needs something else to be whole,
which is compassion. In some sense *The Sutra that Vimalakirti
Speaks* is about making the journey from enlightenment — the
Buddha in the garden — to endarkenment — the large-hearted
bodhisattva on his sickbed — and discovering that, in order to
fully awaken, each needs the other to question, to listen, and to
open to the roaring silence of things.

If you're wondering what the bright needs from the dark,
remember Shariputra's initial dissatisfaction about the way
the world is, his wish that it were different so he could be at
ease. Notice throughout the story the precarious hold on their
enlightenment that some of the garden-dwellers have : they

don't want to be perturbed by Vimalakirti's perturbing questions, they self-righteously reject the flowers (flowers!) that a goddess rains on them a little later in the story. They need a lot of special circumstances to protect their purity, and they're anxious about being defiled. (Consider how many exhortations we receive daily about everything we really should be doing about getting and staying fit, happy, successful, productive, youthful, serene, efficient, attractive, well-organized — which is our secular version of the same thing.) Vimalakirti, in contrast, isn't afraid to go anywhere or to engage with anyone, and that large-hearted courage is one of the great gifts of endarkenment to awakening.

If Vimalakirti embodies endarkenment, it makes a perfect kind of sense that he would be sick, because that's what endarkenment does — it takes us into the shared, common experiences of the sentient world, where by their nature things get complicated. And where they get complicated is also where they get deep and wide, and connected, and enlarging, and full of unexpected grace, if we let them.

In modern terms, we might also think of the dialogue between Manjushri and Vimalakirti as the crucial meeting between conscious and unconscious, or waking and dreaming life. Perhaps we could say that Manjushri is the flash of insight that moves at the lightning speed of synaptic firings in the brain; he has a swift sword that cuts through complication and confusion. Vimalakirti, on the other hand, represents the slower movements of the heart, the idiosyncratic inhale-and-exhale beat of a bloody muscle. He has a remarkable sickbed, upon which he lies down to rest on the vastness.

We know what it's like when mind and heart are laboring separately from each other. The heaviness of a human heart unlightened by insight is often what brings people to meditation. Then, when we begin to have certain kinds of meditation experiences, insight will do what it does, which is run out ahead. That's painful in its own way, because you can see everything so clearly but you can't for the time being feel warmth or tenderness. You have to suffer the discomfort while your heart catches up; if you don't, you become one of those companions on the Way who makes people wonder how someone who's done so much meditating can be such a jerk (except the word is usually something stronger than jerk).

So in each of us Manjushri and Vimalakirti have this grand conversation, looking for a way to move in some kind of sync, even if it's at different speeds. Manjushri's mind is always making discernments about things, and Vimalakirti's heart is embracing them. We want Manjushri's bright clarity *and* we want the soulful depths that endarkenment brings to us.

Bodhisattva Sickness

I am sick because the whole world is sick.

Vimalakirti

In their dialogue, Manjushri and Vimalakirti indirectly respond to Shariputra's lament that the world doesn't feel like a paradise to him. Manjushri asks a series of questions that seem to come out of a desire to fix Vimalakirti's illness. Again, by illness the sutra means any kind of dis-ease, be it physical, emotional, mental, social, cultural, or spiritual — whatever in this tilted world feels tilted in a way that causes us suffering. But for Vimalakirti, dealing with dis-ease isn't simply a matter of eliminating a problem; he's interested in how we can be free in whatever circumstances we find ourselves, wherever we are along the spectrum of sick to well. In his answers to Manjushri's questions, he lays out a process of healing the human heart that takes time, attention, and care.

Without waiting for answers, Manjushri asks Vimalakirti, "Can you bear it?" Then he asks, "Could the treatment be making you worse?" (Anyone who's taken up a spiritual path will wonder at some point whether the treatment is worse than the disease.) Then, "How did you get this?" Next, "How long have you had it?" And finally, "How can it be extinguished?"

Manjushri is the patron saint of experiences that are instant and thoroughgoing, in which everything changes from one moment to the next and it's clear that we're never going to revert to the previous status quo. In his last question he's asking how Vimalakirti's illness can be made to disappear in that way, which isn't necessarily the same thing as how it might be healed; think of the contemporary good death movement, which obviously isn't about not dying, but about dying in a good way. For most of us, awakening is made of a mixture of Manjushri's quantum shifts and Vimalakirti's process of transforming dis-ease into some kind of ease in the midst of uneasy states.

If Manjushri's inquiries are quite familiar to anyone who's been sick, Vimalakirti's responses aren't the ordinary ones : *Oh, I caught the bug that's going around, and I'm drinking lots of fluids.* They aren't even philosophically orthodox : *I am reaping the effects of long-standing karmic conditions having to do with actions in previous lives.* Instead, he responds with these famous words :

> I am sick because the whole world is sick. If everyone's illness were healed, mine would be, too. Why? Because bodhisattvas come into this world of birth and death for the sake of all beings, and part of being in this world of birth and death is getting sick. When everyone is liberated from illness, I will be, too.

"I am sick because the whole world is sick." This is the purest formulation of Vimalakirti's absolute, unquestioned, unmitigated, unbuffered, uncompromised allegiance to this world. I am the world and the world is me; we have one condition.

When the world's heart is breaking, my heart breaks. When the morning star rises, I rise with it. I am the sorrow of the world and its joy, and we share the same fate. To love is to love the world, and to hate is to hate the world. The world's healing is my healing, in which I have an infinitesimal and essential part. It is that simple, that naked and open, that settled in the deepest places, the underground delta where the river of my heart-mind meets the sea of the world's. Here is my condition, out of which everything else flows. When I can touch this without twitching, abide here without fleeing, what naturally flows into me from the sea of the world is *bodhichitta*, the intention toward awakening, because my awakening is the world's awakening. I am waking because the whole world is waking.

What flows into us is the world's yearning, which we experience as our own. The aspiration we feel isn't toward something outside itself; the aspiration, the yearning, is it. When we can touch this without twitching, abide here without fleeing, a bodhisattva begins to be born. Bodhisattvas give birth to themselves, something that happens every time a person like one of us does a couple of things. First, you find arising in your heart the intention to awaken, so that you can discover what you uniquely do that's helpful in the world; that's bodhichitta. And then you make the commitment known as the bodhisattva vow to put that intention at the center of your life.

A bodhisattva is born not by becoming instantly and completely awake and skillful at everything, constantly bestowing wonderful gifts on others, but simply by having the willingness to put this commitment at the center. And then spending the rest of your life figuring out what that means, provisionally, imperfectly, every day. This is how a bodhisattva — a yearning, an intention — enters the world of birth and death for the sake of all beings. We begin, and then the birth is midwifed by our family, our loved ones, our coworkers, our companions on the Way.

Vimalakirti continues, "Part of being in this world of birth and death is getting sick." We live in a world of change and impermanence, of coming and going, rising and falling, birth and death. Because we live in that kind of world, we're constantly experiencing cycles that include arcs of growth, and also of decay. Illness and the other arcs of unbecoming are just as natural as the arcs of healing and becoming. This is the nature of the lives we lead.

Vimalakirti finishes by saying, "When everyone is liberated from illness, I will be, too." I hear in this a fundamental allegiance to life as it is. I'm like this because the world is like this. You're like this because the world is like this. If the world changed and we were able to release ourselves from illness, none of us would be ill anymore. But as long as we can't, as long as we're still in the process, I'm in, too.

Pretending to be Sick

See how vast and wide the world is. Why do you get up
and get dressed at the sound of the morning bell?

Yunmen

The sutra mentions at the beginning that Vimalakirti is
only pretending to be sick, using skillful means in order to
teach others. The Buddhist concept of skillful means is a tricky
one; it's possible to make big, consequential mistakes when you
believe you know how to bend your message, circumstances,
and other people in the service of (your idea of) helpfulness.
And realizing that you're on the other end of someone else's
attempt at skillful means can sometimes just feel icky. The
skillful means interpretation feels a bit pious to me, or like the
sutra-makers are trying to distance themselves from something
they find unsettling in Vimalakirti's message. Anyway, there
are some less orthodox and perhaps more fruitful ways of
looking at this 'pretending.'

That Vimalakirti might be pretending to be sick is reminiscent of something the Chan teacher Huangbo says : "Teaching

Chan is like casting fake pearls before people pretending to be beggars." Huangbo knows that he's offering his 'pearls of wisdom' to people already in possession of the greatest jewel, the awakening inherent in each of us. In other words, whatever our circumstances, even if we're in need or ill, that doesn't make us essentially beggars or sick people; it makes us beings in a world that includes poverty, disease, and many other sorrows. It's a call to see, in addition to wounds and scars, the small glow of awakening in each of our bellies.

The invitation is to open some space between the natural condition of being alive in a world of birth and death, and an unchanging identification with some aspect of that condition. The nature of being alive in such a world is to be a little tilted, because the world is tilted. That's different from saying that your identity is most significantly the particular way you're tilted. I've lived with a fairly serious chronic health condition, and I can remember early on having to decide whether I was going to go through life as the sick girl, which is how I thought of it. That would have been an identification with my condition, taking one fact of my life, putting it at the center, and hitching everything else up to that tethering post.

Vimalakirti's alternative is to let your vow of awakening settle at the center instead. Over time the vow spreads out into a kind of field, and everything from the fleeting moments to the longstanding circumstances of your life will arise in that field, and the vow will help hold them. This field tends to have fewer fortifications linked by deep grooves of habit, more spacious views, and a milder climate on most days.

Hanging out in such a field can bring ease, and ease can bring openness. The bodhisattva of compassion is called Guanyin in Chinese, which means Listens. This vow we're talking about is her vow, and so it calls us to listen with a simple heart to our kin of all kinds when they speak, roar, cry, and whisper about the sorrows of a tilted world. Held together by scars and radiance, all of us. Often in need, all of us, and sometimes some of us in great need. The filaments that connect us vibrating with prayers and exhortations. The vow at the center, the small glow in our bellies, listening, sending out its own filaments in reply.

It's starting to go a bit dreamlike and mysterious inside this 'pretending.' Yunmen, another Chan teacher, asks a question that takes us further along that path : "See how vast and wide the world is. Why do you get up and get dressed at the sound of the morning bell?" Why, in the midst of the unfathomable vastness, do you get up every morning when the alarm goes off and start another ordinary day? Why do I come out of the deep space of sleep every morning to put on my human skin and go out to live a human life?

Maybe it's because each of us is the vastness manifesting in a particular way. You're this person, I'm that person, there are the bird persons under the eaves and the ground cover persons just beginning to spread in the courtyard. We put on our clothes when the alarm goes off because, for another day, we accept the invitation to be the vastness taking this form, and we'll try not to be stingy about it. We'll 'pretend' to be human beings in our human being skins, not in the sense of a false performance but remembering that we're both born and unborn, named and unnamed — human and everything else in the universe, too. There's a sense of play about this : the performance today is heavily flavored by memories of childhood summers at the beach or comically ramifying lists of tasks, or it is stained and dyed by silence.

In a koan from the *Book of Serenity*, the Chan teacher Dongshan is dying, and a monastic asks him, "You're unwell. Is there someone, after all, who isn't sick?" Is there an aspect of you unaffected by illness? Is there some eternal buddha nature part of you that isn't experiencing the sickness you're experiencing?

Dongshan says, "There is."

So the monastic asks, "Does the one who isn't sick take care of you?" That's a natural way to think about it : if there's something we believe in, like buddha nature or God or Goddess or whatever we identify as that-which-is-not-sick, do we find consolation and comfort there? Are we being taken care of by the not-sickness of the universe?

But Dongshan says the opposite : "I'm actually taking care of that one." By being sick, I'm taking care of that one who is not sick. In other words, the life I have been given is shaped like this right now. Even when it's hard, it's an extraordinary gift, the vastness swirling into form to experience itself like this, like me, and in exchange I'm living my life as generously as I can.

The monastic asks, "What's it like when you take care of that one?"

Dongshan says, "Then I don't see that there is any illness." I might be sick, but I don't have preconceived ideas about what illness is. I'm not going to start from the position that illness is a failure of life to go as it should, or that it's some kind of gift. Let me be sick and find out what it means.

Once when a particularly bad patch of illness stretched on for months, I'd wake in the morning and sometimes, just for a moment, I was in the sweet, calm space before the illness constellated around me, and I could remember what not-sick was like. Then the symptoms would start blinking, and I'd realize that it was going to be another long, challenging day. I'd stumble out of bed, make tea, and weep. Both things were true, the sweetness of a moment of physical ease and the weeping. Denying neither of them, living them both as uncomplicatedly as I was able, was what I could do those days to care for that one, to stay close to the vow.

Unbeguiled by the lure of skillful means, I marvel instead as my hand figures out, moment by moment, what it means to be a hand, and my heart learns what a heart is on a sunny morning after days of fog. Are they, am I, pretending? Not exactly, but sort of, if pretending means a series of assays and approximations, one not-knowing flowing into another, with lots of pauses to listen. Outside my window, are subatomic particles pretending to be trees? The world isn't only a dream, but it is, in part. How do we tend to a dream?

Small Compassion

I saw you fall, so I'm helping.
Pang Lingzhao[15]

Let's pause for a moment to consider that if ever a word were in need of emergency resuscitation, it's compassion. It's gotten so tangled up in our ideas about what we think we ought to be feeling and doing and how we imagine we fall short that we'd be forgiven for taking against it. And to the extent we feel aversive toward it, we stop engaging with it in a lively way, and it goes generic. Just what does compassion mean anymore, exactly? Well, this sutra has some bracingly uncommon ideas about that, so perhaps it's just the tonic our semi-comatose word needs.

When Manjushri asks about his illness, Vimalakirti replies, "My illness comes from great compassion." When something is called 'great' in the Chinese philosophical tradition, it's more than an adjective of praise or ranking. Things are simultane-

---

15   This comes from a koan about a young woman who, when she sees her father trip and fall, throws herself down next to him

ously seen from both great and small perspectives, which are equally important.

Vimalakirti is engaged in small compassion all the time, if we think of small compassion as the detailed, the particular, the local. It's the ways we live and interact in this fragile zone of earth and sky that includes this rocky planet, the thin layer of organic matter under our feet, and the surrounding air. We in our human flesh attempt to deal in decent and helpful ways with the flesh of others : other humans, other animals; the flesh of plants; even the flesh of nuclear reactors. We're using our embodiedness, our materiality, to affect the embodiedness and materiality of others, flesh on flesh. That's the small view of compassion — and it's no small thing.

Vimalakirti walks the back streets and dark alleys of the city outside of which the Buddha is encamped. He's going places where many of the Buddha's disciples wouldn't, because they're afraid, as much for their spiritual as their physical safety. They think that to walk those streets — to see what you would see and engage with what you would engage with in those places — represents a threat to their deepest spiritual desire : to be released from this life between earth and sky, which to them seems like a realm of great suffering. Vimalakirti isn't afraid in that way. In fact, quite the opposite : his particular expression of bodhisattva is willing to go anywhere, and to extend a hand wherever it's possible to do so. And not only is he doing that, but it isn't bothering him. He's sick but he isn't suffering, and that's an important distinction.

When I amplify the story of Vimalakirti, I wonder : What happened on his way through those difficult places? Did he catch tuberculosis? Was he beaten up? What might have been the proximate cause of his illness? Whatever happened, it doesn't translate into suffering, because he's doing what he believes is the essential thing to do. That essential thing isn't to go out and deliberately throw himself in the path of getting sick or injured, but to accept that to be alive is to get dinged up. How many of us will make it through life without scars and antibodies, painful memories and regrets? The root of small compassion is to understand that there's no escaping such things, only a question of how we acquire them : in service to what?

Vimalakirti's illness, like all our dings if we let them, put us in touch with how most people live. Above my desk is something Eleanor Roosevelt said : "Most of the work in the world is done by people who weren't feeling very well that day." Vimalakirti's courage, and ours, bring us into situations where we might be helpful. It seems obvious to say it, but we are most helpful where people — and animals, and plants, and nuclear reactors — are in trouble.

How is he able to engage in these small, radiant acts of compassion, and even get sick from doing so, but not suffer? How does he keep from crossing that gap that's so easy to cross? What's the view that helps us to acts of risky generosity that don't have suffering as their inevitable result? This is where we get into the realm of great compassion, which isn't a different form of compassion, but a different way of looking at it.

Let us, sometimes-frightened disciples, pause again for a small moment of small compassion amongst ourselves. Vimalakirti is an astonishing figure, a mythic one. That means he's larger than life and more of just about everything, most likely, than we could imagine for ourselves. So what do we do with that? Do we reject it as so idealized as to be meaningless or oppressive, as we might with compassion? Or can we think of him as an ally, a protector, a reminder of the potential each of us is gestating? Can we imagine him not as some carnival figure to measure ourselves against but as the force of the world turning its mercy toward us? Vimalakirti is the kind words that saved your life once, the sunrise that started your heart healing, the pain that stopped you in your tracks when you needed to stop. Can we see him shining with the reflected light of all our aspirations toward awakening? When I do that, a huge tenderness rises in me, for your aspirations, for my aspirations, for the world's bottomless longing to awaken.

Great Compassion

My illness comes from great compassion.

Vimalakirti

Small compassion is made up of all the tender, everyday, spontaneous, local, humble things we do for each other. Great compassion is, really, the compassion the universe enacted when it gave birth to itself, gave birth to each of us; it's the reverberations throughout time and space of that first unfathomable gift. Small compassions are the way we give voice and flesh to that original vow, the way we reproduce the gift in the actual moments of our actual lives.

Okay, yikes. Maybe it'd be easier to just hoist compassion back onto the gurney. But adding this understanding to the mix can be helpful, because it gives context and perspective : we are not the manufacturers of compassion, or the ones responsible for it; it's already everywhere around us, and pretty much our job is to find ways to ride its currents. Earlier we talked about how endarkenment is letting your heart be broken open by the world, and in a sense that's small (tender, everday, spontaneous, local, humble) endarkenment. An awareness of the fundamentally unknowable mystery, the unfathomable gift at the heart of *everything*, is great endarkenment.

Over the next few chapters of the sutra, Vimalakirti speaks about how having this large context and perspective affects our daily enactments of small compassion. After centuries of Buddhist treatises on the practices leading to enlightenment, Vimalakirti lays out one of the first drafts of the practices of endarkenment.

Manjushri wants Vimalakirti to explain what he means by saying that his illness comes from great compassion, so he asks three questions. First, "What is compassion?"

Vimalakirti answers, "Completely share whatever good you do with everyone." He's already said, "I am sick because the whole world is sick," which is one way of saying that he shares in the condition of all beings. Now he's showing the other side : and I share *my* condition with all beings, through my actions.

There's an exchange going on : you let the world affect you, experiencing compassion first as a willingness to be pierced by the poignant blade of life. And you allow yourself to have an effect, letting what is good in you flow from that pierced heart to others.

When Vimalakirti says that compassion is completely sharing whatever good you do, there's an emphasis on what you *do* more than how you feel. Often we assign compassion to the feeling realm : faced with suffering, we feel sorrow, righteous indignation, love, or pity; or we're overwhelmed, numb, helpless. Whatever the case, we assume that compassion arises from how we feel, or cannot arise if we're not in the right frame of mind. From the view of great compassion, how you feel doesn't necessarily have anything to do with what you do, and what you do is the important thing.

Vimalakirti particularly calls out "a sentimental view of great compassion," which "creates weariness and aversion toward the world of birth and death." A sentimental view of compassion is something like pity — *Oh, poor you* — and it's a short leap from *Poor you!* to *Bad world!* This is another expression of Vimalakirti's profound allegiance to our tilty life : be concerned, care, put yourself out, without making the world bad. It's tough to be helpful when your energy is bound up in a fight with life for being life. Vimalakirti advises us to put outrage and disappointment down and instead take up the impossible vow to love the world, no matter what.

But doesn't intention matter? If you're helping someone, doesn't it make a difference whether you're sympathetic or angry, accepting or judgmental? Of course it does; it's likely to stain and dye the event. But compassion is something deeper than any state, even empathy; if your intention is to be empathetic, whatever you do is really an act of empathy. That's a noble thing and to be praised but not identical with compassion, which is the expression of a different intention, our bodhichitta. When our actions arise from there, our feeling states might accompany our desire for the world to awaken, but they can't replace it or block it.

The startling suggestion is that you don't have to feel empathy or even to understand in order to be compassionate. It's possible to be furious with someone, or indifferent, and still be compassionate. How you act doesn't have to be directly connected to your opinion about the situation, and you don't have to wait to act until your feelings line up the way you think they should. Here's this ancient, strange voice suggesting a different way to think about where our allegiances lie : these days we often place great value on virtues like authenticity and speaking our truth, but anyone who's stayed up all night with a sick child after an exhausting day understands that sometimes compassion calls us to an allegiance beyond our immediate self-oriented concerns, and authenticity and truth are best expressed by a cool cloth on a hot forehead in the early hours of the morning.

What Vimalakirti proposes, I believe, is a process for healing the human heart. It might seem strange to say that compassion is really more about what we do than about how we feel, and then to say that this is a process of healing the heart. Vimalakirti is suggesting that we settle the desire, longing, passion, or intention of bodhichitta in the middle of our lives, and begin. We're going to make mistakes and hit dead ends along the way, so it'll be easier if we lighten the load by putting some things down, which mostly relate to not privileging our feeling states above all else.

Huangbo says, "Feeling compassion is knowing that there's no one to be saved." In other words, there aren't people and things fundamentally different from you, falling into the category of 'those who need to be saved,' yourself falling into the category of 'the one who's doing the saving.' We are all here in this thin band of life between rock and space, and we lift each other up and we push each other down, and we help, and we don't help, and we receive help, and it goes around and around. Sometimes we offer compassion and sometimes we receive it, and often those two things are so intimately intertwined it's hard to tell one from the other. To put it in koan terms, sometimes you're the host and sometimes you're the guest. There's humility in this understanding, and perhaps a bit of relief. Which of many possible bodhisattvas are you in this situation? What bend does your intention towards awakening take? Which of many possible bodhisattvas are you reaching your hand out to?

We're moving with Vimalakirti toward living openheartedly in the presence of suffering. When our orientation shifts in this way, we're beginning a process that isn't going to be fully realized at the start. Compassion is first a vow, an intention, a commitment. That's not just preparing for compassion; that's already compassion, as is working toward responding in ways that are helpful, regardless of how you feel, to whatever extent you can. The willingness to share whatever good you have, even without complete sympathy or understanding, is full-blown compassion, because it *is* the good you have, and that's what full-blown means; because it's as much as you can do, it's all of it.

Vimalakirti reminds us that compassion isn't a project of the ego, focused on reaping the rewards of doing the right thing, but on sharing whatever is good in us, whatever skills and arts we have, whatever largeness we possess, however we can be helpful — over and over again. The good in us belongs not to ourselves, but to the world; it is a migratory bird that for a moment has come to rest in us, which we shelter and feed and send on its way.

The strategies the ego employs to wrest our attention from the work at hand and back to itself — stances like self-righteousness, judgment, or guilt, and actions like squandering our resources and depleting our energy — work against compassion great and small. We know the troubles that self-centeredness can kick up in the realm of helpfulness and kindness, but we can also get into trouble if we tilt too far in the other direction, overriding our own capacities. Fortunately the remedy for this is pretty simple : include yourself in the field of your compassion. Remember that you aren't special in either direction, deserving extra or unworthy of enough; extend the same bodhisattva hand to yourself that you would to someone else. Encouraging, supporting, nourishing, protecting, and challenging the good in us are all part of taking care of that good, which is our lovely responsibility to do.

Comfort

Manjushri asks Vimalakirti, "How should a bodhisattva
comfort bodhisattvas who are ill?"

Manjushri is interested in how the vast perspective of great
compassion affects what we do, and so he asks, "How should a
bodhisattva comfort bodhisattvas who are ill?"

Vimalakirti replies, "Remind them that the body is impermanent, but don't suggest that as a result you should repudiate
the body."

How *should* we feel about our mortal bodies, especially when
they're being particularly mortal? Once Dongshan was asked,
"Among the three bodies of the Buddha,[16] what body doesn't
fall into categories?" In other words, what's the body that you
can't really characterize, that doesn't fall into our habitual ways
of seeing things?

Dongshan replied, "I am always intimate with it." This

---

16 The *trikaya* : *nirmanakaya* (the material body and world), *sambhogakaya*
(the dream body and world), and *dharmakaya* (the body and world of the
vastness)

body is defined by your intimacy with it rather than by your opinions about its condition. It is made of that intimacy, which is what great compassion feels like up close, against your skin. What does it mean to be intimate with your body, in whatever its condition or state? This begins with letting your body reveal its condition to you, without interrupting with preconceptions and judgments or jumping too early to fixes.

In his answer, Vimalakirti is breaking the early Buddhist bond between impermanence and aversion, the idea that because things are unstable and subject to death, we should mistrust and reject them. If impermanence is the cause of a lot of pain and suffering, it also means that we can do something about that, because things are always in flux — maybe over years or generations or geological ages, but still by their nature capable of change. When Vimalakirti says, "Completely share whatever good you do with everyone," he's saying that when we're confronted with impermanence and difficulty, our job is to bring a kind of grace into the world, the awareness of the possibility of change.

The second way that a bodhisattva should comfort bodhisattvas who are ill, according to Vimalakirti, is to "remind them that the body suffers, but don't suggest that as a result you should strive for nirvana." This is another way of saying the same thing : yes, the body suffers, but we shouldn't be trying to transcend it; the way to deal with suffering is to learn to live openheartedly in its presence, and the entire sutra is about how to do that.

The third way we should comfort bodhisattvas who are ill is to "remind them that the body is without self, but suggest that you should help others anyway." If you don't have a self, what's the point of trying to help you? This is a pernicious distortion of the Way : the implication of selflessness isn't that no one is suffering; it's that there are no comfortable, distancing categories of giver, given to, and gift, no safe corralling of suffering 'over there.' Respond to the suffering, and the metaphysics will take care of itself.

The fourth is : "Remind them that the body is serene in its emptiness, but don't teach that it is ultimately extinguished." This one, as I understand it, is about the vast aspect of the body (the dharmakaya), utterly eternal and unrippled, which isn't awaiting us in nirvana because we already have it. You don't have to transcend or extinguish anything (ouch!) to obtain serenity : may you, on behalf of the world, discover it even in pain, even in difficulty, and let it ripple.

The fifth response is more contrarian advice : "Explain that you should regret your former transgressions, but don't consign them to the past. Use your own illness to sympathize with the illness of others." In other words, do *not* let bygones be bygones, as far as you're concerned. Use your own wounds and the mistakes you've made to open your heart so that you can better comfort others in their distress. If you hold a living recognition of the ways you've messed up and are capable of messing up, it softens your attitude toward others and brings out your natural ability to understand and forgive.

You might have noticed that Vimalakirti often answers Manjushri's questions by suggesting what you shouldn't do, without telling you what you ought to do instead. I don't think that's an accident. In the koan tradition, which takes Vimalakirti as one of its founding ancestors even if he didn't know it, what needs clearing away to make space for our bodhichitta looks pretty much the same from person to person. Each of us might have our own baroque variations, but, fundamentally, the list of things that challenge our awakening is pretty universal.

Once the clearing away has begun, *you* have to discover what comes next. This tradition will tell you what to put down, but it won't tell you what to pick up instead. That's your exploration, and what a glorious exploration! There are no recipes or directives, because from the perspective of this tradition, there couldn't be. What I pick up isn't necessarily what's right for you to pick up. Whatever each of us does that is good — whatever skills, whatever arts, whatever qualities of character each of us has — that's what we do.

Vimalakirti is saying that if you do these things that are good for other people, it's also going to mend your heart. Here is a way to be intimate with your own body, heart, and mind; find the peace already within yourself; and even to accept your own wounds and idiosyncrasies, which can bring understanding and forgiveness for yourself and others.

There's an implied commitment to do this work so that what flows from you will have more 'good' about it. What does 'good' mean when we're speaking of compassion? Probably something like brave, willing to take chances and be wrong, noticing what effect our actions have and adjusting accordingly. If 'good' is most importantly a synonym for 'helpful,' we're signing up for trying to understand what 'helpful' means. The next two exchanges between Manjushri and Vimalakirti speak to this.

Renunciation

Manjushri asks, "What is renunciation?"
Vimalakirti replies, "No expectations about the blessings
that are generated."

Awhile ago Manjushri began asking Vimalakirti a series
of questions about illness coming from great compassion. His
first question was, "What is compassion?" Now his question
is, "What is renunciation?" In most of the Asian languages in
which Buddhism grew, 'renunciation' has a different flavor
than it does in English. When westerners talk about renunciation, we tend to emphasize what you're giving up : you
renounce some thing, activity, or habit, and you usually have a
reason for doing so. You think it's bad for you, you're demon-
strating your sincerity, you're doing some kind of penance, or
you think it's immoral to go on doing what you're doing. In
the countries of Buddhism's original development, the idea
of renunciation includes what is made possible by putting
something down and clearing the space. The focus is on what's
coming rather than what's going.

Vimalakirti suggests that if compassion is freely giving

what is good in us to others, the way to make the freest gift possible is to renounce our opinions about, and even our fondest hopes for, the effects of what we offer. The *Bhagavad Gita*[17] agrees : "You have a right to your actions but never to the fruits of your actions ... Act without any thought of results, open to success or failure." Daoists expressed a similar idea in the *Daodejing*[18] : "Do your work, then step back — the only path to serenity."

If we have a powerful need to quickly solve the seemingly overwhelming problems of our time, that's probably going to land us somewhere on the spectrum between disappointment and despair. Vimalakirti inquires about how it would be if we put bodhichitta at the center and act from that, without a guarantee that our actions will take care of whatever needs we bring to the situation. What if we do it because we can't imagine not doing it, no matter what? Do our small and incomplete offerings have value, too?

No one in Vimalakirti's room would argue against giving up self-centered, in-denial, ruled-by-greed-hatred-and-ignorance ways of being in the world. And as we do, maybe it's natural that we allow ourselves to be so deeply pierced by the troubles of the world that we despair for awhile; that might even be the necessary antidote to the previous problem. But Vimalakirti is saying that you can't stop there, because, first of all, if we have bodhichitta at the center, our motivating energy is to be helpful, and it's difficult to be helpful from a position of despair. Despair is destructive to our intention and damaging

---

17 A section of the sprawling Indian classic *Mahabharata*, from around the same time as early Buddhist literature

18 The early classic of Daoism, sometimes romanized as *Tao Te Ching*, also from around the same time

to our hearts. And second, it's partial. If we're going to see what's missing in the world, what we're failing to do, we should also see the small blessings of what is getting done. They're here, and they're real.

Joy

Manjushri asks, "What is joy?"
Vimalakirti replies, "If there is benefit, rejoice without regret."

Though we've released our grip on the outcome of our actions, if good things result, please be unreservedly happy about that. You have the intention to be helpful — the difficulties of the world flow in — you give whatever you have that's good — that flows back into the world. If there's some benefit, some small moment of relief, reconciliation, or refreshment that comes out of that, let *that* flow back in to you, so that the gift continues to circulate. What you've renounced is the drive for a certain outcome, arising from your own needs; what you've gained is a willingness to be delighted.

Rejoicing without regret means rejoicing completely in what's happened without keeping account of all the things that haven't. Regret is about what hasn't been done and how much else there is to do. Earlier Vimalakirti says, "If everyone is released from illness, I am no longer ill." If there is benefit, if there is blessing, if for just a moment in a tiny, local corner of the world something good happens, in that moment living beings are released from pain, and I share in that release. If I join them in sorrow and suffering, I join them too in healing.

Sometimes, when there's so much that's hard in the world, joy can feel like a betrayal of those who are suffering. Sometimes it's more difficult to open to happiness than to sorrow. Being not-two means simply responding to what's actually happening : if it's something sorrowful, you feel sorrow, something joyful, joy. Vimalakirti's absolute, unquestioned, unmitigated, unbuffered, uncompromised allegiance to this world includes the rare, the just-born, the glinting and swaying and swooping, the shy smile and the sudden guffaw, pirouettes and bursts of song, bright eyes, swelling chests, and reaching arms.

The Goddess in the Room

Flowers Fall

Everything that exists is a manifestation of liberation.

the Goddess

One of the many extraordinary things about Vimalakirti's room is the Goddess who's been living here for twelve years. She's the only major figure in the sutra who is described rather than named, which is often the case with female Buddhist characters, like the *naga* princess[19] and the innkeeper at Hara Station.[20] She's also the only figure raised alongside Vimalakirti who doesn't represent an apparent duality with him, let alone tension or disagreement; though their styles are different, they seem to be in perfect accord.

When the Goddess sees this assembly of 32,000 souls and hears the conversation going on, she makes herself visible and showers flowers on everyone. The flowers rain down upon

---

19 Nagas are mythological snake-dragon hybrids with supernatural powers

20 The nameless innkeeper appears in a story with the eighteenth-century Japanese koan teacher Hakuin

two kinds of people : bodhisattvas and some of the disciples of the Buddha. The sutra refers to these disciples as the private buddhas, because they think of enlightenment as a personal and individual experience they're pursuing for themselves. One of the subtexts throughout the story is a contrast between these private buddhas and the bodhisattvas, who yearn for awakening so that they can help others awaken. Note that we're immediately back in the realm of dualities.

The flowers fall softly to the ground around the bodhisattvas, but they stick to the private buddhas. The private buddhas believe that because they're ascetics they shouldn't be wearing flowers, so they try to pick them off. But the flowers won't be dislodged, even when the disciples turn on them the supernatural powers they've acquired through meditation. Pause for a moment to absorb this image : a group of accomplished practitioners turning the force of their accumulated prajna to defend against a soft shower of blossoms. Their defeat catches everyone by surprise, including Shariputra.

The Goddess turns to Shariputra and asks, "Why would you try to remove the flowers?"

Shariputra answers, "Because these flowers are contrary to the teachings." He's referring to the fact that monastics are forbidden to adorn themselves.

The Goddess replies, "Don't say that these flowers are contrary to the teachings. They make no such discrimination for or against the teachings, or anything else; you're the one generating discriminative thoughts. If someone like you who's left the householder's life to follow the Buddha makes that kind of discrimination, *that* is what is contrary to the teachings."

Here is the Goddess' first teaching, about views and duality and reality. A physicist once said that with the Big Bang, an almost infinite multiplicity of viewpoints was created, which is an interesting way of looking at what the universe is. Where we get into trouble is if we confuse our particular view with reality. In the immortal words of Daniel Patrick Moynihan, "You are entitled to your own opinions, but you are not entitled to your own facts." It might turn out that we have a more-or-less realistic view of the flowers, and it might turn out that we don't. The important thing is to recognize that what we have is a view, and views are provisional and impermanent; they rise and fall. We can explore a view, and it ought to be subject to new evidence. At any given moment it's our best guess, which is pretty much what we get in this life. The Goddess is reminding us that duality doesn't actually exist in the world around us : it exists in our minds. Duality is something our mind *does* with the world.

Shariputra asks the Goddess how long she's been in this room, and she replies that she's been there as long as he's been free. It's another moment that reveals Vimalakirti's room as the space of awakening within each of us. But when she asks him how long that is, he won't answer. She asks him why, and he says, "Liberation cannot be spoken of in words, and so I don't know what I can say to you." This sounds like Zen 101 : Zen is a special transmission outside the scriptures, not dependent on words.

The Goddess responds, "Words and speech are manifestations of liberation." She's implying that when you say that liberation can't be spoken of, you're making words special — in this case, specially bad — instead of realizing that words are as good, bad, capable of illuminating, and capable of misuse as anything else. It all depends on what you do with them.

She then goes a step further : "Everything that exists is a manifestation of liberation."

Shariputra asks what might seem like the obvious question : "Isn't liberation detachment from greed, aggression, and denial?" Isn't spiritual practice about sorting between things that get us closer to liberation and things that move us further away?

But nonduality means we can't have two piles of anything; there's only one pile, and everything in it is a manifestation of liberation. The koans say over and over again that anything, however apparently trivial or noxious, can become an occasion for our awakening — just as each of us, however trivial or noxious we might feel, can become that occasion for someone else. I've been brought a crushed beer can that woke somebody up, and taken outside to see the one rock in a landscape of rocks that rose to fetch someone else. Everything comes from the same dark, everything is filled with the same light.

Which isn't to say that everything is completed just yet; there is still more horror and viciousness than it's possible almost to bear. But aren't those the very things most in need of inclusion in this agonizingly slow, grievously uneven awakening? The move from private buddha to bodhisattva means that we vow to wake up *in* the world, *for* the world, and *with* the world; everything partakes in our dream of awakening.

Sometimes it's something else that seems like it ought to be in the not-liberation pile, and sometimes it can feel as though you yourself are buried there. A koan says, "Under a shadowless tree, the boat where people gather." This is the community ferryboat, and we're all on it together, crossing to the other shore. Sometimes you really know you're on the boat, and sometimes it can feel that you're not. But there's no such thing as being off the boat. Everything you encounter and every state you're in, whether it's a good or bad or indifferent day, is on the boat; for each of us as well as for the world, everything is part of the dream of awakening.

Once again, what changes is our perception, our ability to know and experience that. Instead of asking about how to get back on the boat when we feel as though we're off, we're asking why we're not feeling the planks under our feet. How can you return to intimacy with what's already true? Coming up next, the Goddess has some interesting things to say about that.

Self-Obsession & Its Transformation

Buddhahood is passion and passion is buddhahood.
                                        Zhaozhou

The Goddess shocks Shariputra by saying, "The buddhas only say to self-obsessed people that detachment from greed, aggression, and denial is liberation. For those who aren't self-obsessed, the buddhas say that the very essence of greed, aggression, and denial is liberation."

First of all, let's assume that we're going to take the advice of the sutra and refrain from making piles of good (not self-obsessed) and bad (self-obsessed) about this. We're going to look at self-obsessed and not self-obsessed as territories we walk through at different points in our lives. Perhaps we tend over time from more self-obsession to less self-obsession; perhaps there are places where we're not self-obsessed anymore, while there are other places where we're still deeply engaged with self-obsession. And let's also assume that self-obsession involves more than focusing on the concerns of the self, which is an ordinary part of life; we've tipped into obsession when the focus is consuming enough that it causes suffering for ourselves and others.

If we don't make good and bad about that, the first question is a simple self-diagnosis : Am I self-obsessed, and if so, where? This is important because the treatment that's offered differs depending on the diagnosis, and we want the medicine most likely to help us. How do you discern whether you're self-obsessed?

In general terms, self-obsession can mean being full of greed, aggression, and denial that's squirting out of you onto everybody else, and you have justifications for why that's okay. You have a strong commitment to the self and its concerns, at the expense of others. It can also mean that you're desperately unhappy about your greed, aggression, and denial, and are always monitoring and trying to fix them. You have a strong commitment to preoccupation with your unhappiness. A third form of self-obsession is spending a lot of your time and energy trying to avoid greed, aggression, and denial in the world around you, because it's scary or it hurts. You have a strong commitment to a self that needs protection from the world; the problem with that, from the perspective of the sutra, is that it puts you in an aversive or a defensive relationship with the world.

If you're tending toward any of these forms of self-obsession, the first phase of goddess-approved treatment is some detachment : get some distance and perspective, and learn to dis-identify with your states and conditions. This sutra about nonduality is saying that there is such a thing as false oneness, such as identifying too closely with our states and our views about our states.

Here's a series of meditations that might illustrate this :

First, after you've sat for a bit, say to yourself, *I had a
_____ childhood*. Fill in the blank with whatever arises and
notice what that's like. Spend a few minutes with it. Then drop
the adjective : *I had a childhood*. What happens? Spend a few
minutes more with that. Finally, pull the camera back even
further : *There was a childhood*. What's that like? Let it sink in,
permeating your meditation without too much thinking about
it. Does your feeling toward that childhood change? Often,
when we can breathe even a little bit of space into our habits of
mind, the false unity is broken, freeing us, if only for a moment
at first, from the trance of self-obsession.

It's quite a moment when you realize that even your
afflictive emotions don't have to be a problem in and of themselves; the problem comes with self-obsession, when you think
your negative emotions are the most important thing, and you
let them take over. With some detachment we can let them rise
and fall along with everything else that's rising and falling in
the field, seeing them in their proper proportion to the whole
— which is generally pretty insignificant, and, eventually, a lot
less interesting than what else is going on.

We don't have to eradicate or transform or scold them,
or feel terribly guilty about them; we don't have to revel in
or indulge them, or be miserable about them, or be miserable
about our misery. We just have to be not-obsessed with them,
noticing what else is going on, noticing that we're not feeling as
committed to them as we once were, realizing with relief that
it's quite possible to let them pass by without grabbing onto
them and throttling them into life.

We do want to be aware of not confusing the method
with the goal : detachment is a *method* that works to antidote
a particular problem, not the reason we're practicing. At a

certain point, you're going to want to detach from detachment, as it were. The gifts of detachment are the moments and then weeks and years that are not self-obsessed, and *they* are the reason to practice, because they open us to the world, and the world to us.

Now comes phase two of the treatment, which is, as the Goddess says, for those who are not self-obsessed — or, more realistically, to the extent that we're not self-obsessed, in the places where we're not self-obsessed. In phase one we've gotten a more spacious, objective relationship with our struggles, and then in phase two we go right back toward those very struggles that have seemed so hard to include in the pile of liberation.

It turns out that our afflictive emotions are more than not-a-problem : their essence *is* liberation, as is the essence of everything that is. Buddha nature pervades the universe, and your anger is as much a possible occasion of awakening as the surprise appearance of cherry blossoms on a mountain path. Which isn't to give us license to go around being furious all the time, but to invite us, when anger comes, to become intimate with it. (A significant byproduct of turning inward towards the anger is that we don't spill it out so readily on the world around us, for which the world is grateful.) In the koan tradition there's a lot of affection for surprise, the interruption of habit, and even shock, and emotions like anger are particularly good at the kind of intimacy that pulls the rug out from under you. When you're so angry you're seeing red, what if you sit right there in the red? Is there a gap that opens up with wondering, *Who's angry?* The answer might surprise you, and it might tumble you right through that gap into the vastness itself.

Over time, the places that have been hard for us become

less like unhealed wounds and more like the ankle that's weak because it's been sprained a few times. You know that if you find yourself on a certain kind of uneven ground, you're likely to turn your ankle. So when you encounter something that touches a tender place, you understand that the sprained ankle of your heart just went out from under you. This is a tenderer, less reactive relationship with your self, which tends toward a tenderer, less reactive relationship with everything else.

Still, how can it be that the sore places in our hearts and what we do that causes suffering are manifestations of liberation? First, because it's in coming into relationship with them, in feeling the sorrow and disappointment of them, that our hearts get cracked open, and there is no awakening without the heart getting cracked open. Awakening is an activity of the heart-mind rather than the mind alone, and if you leave the heart out, you've got the private buddha trying to keep herself safe from difficulty or defilement, succeeding in keeping herself safe from awakening.

And second, because the dream of awakening includes everything; there's nothing outside it, nothing that's not-awakening. Everything is waking up together, not uniformly or all at once, but together. Is there anything we'd more gladly see transformed by awakening than greed, aggression, and denial, cruelty and indifference and selfishness? Would we try to leave them out, even if including them makes our own awakening seem more complicated in the short term? Could it possibly be true that the trap door into the vastness exists only under some moments and not others? That awakening is conditional? And are you ready to bet the farm that you can decide which moments to embrace, and which to repudiate?

One Body

All things are like that :
not existing, and yet not *not* existing.
                                                the Goddess

After awhile, the conversation between the Goddess and
Shariputra moves into the relationship between nonduality and
gender. Shariputra asks why, if she's so wise and can perform
magic, the Goddess doesn't transform her female body into a
male one. The question contains a cultural assumption of that
time and place, and also, I'm sorry to say, of Buddhism for
most of its history : only men could become enlightened; the
best a woman could hope for was rebirth as a man. The sutra
addresses this kind of view head-on and dismantles it.

The Goddess says, "For the past twelve years I've looked
for the essence of femaleness, but I've discovered that it can't
be found. So what is there to transform? It's as if a magician
conjured up a phantom woman. If someone asks the phantom,
'Why don't you transform your female body?' would that
person's question be a reasonable one?"

Shariputra replies, "No, it wouldn't. Phantoms have no

fixed form, so what can you change?"

The Goddess says, "Everything is like that; nothing has a fixed form. So why would you ask about transforming my female body?"

The Goddess is expressing the radical message of Mahayana Buddhism for that time and place, which is that there is no place we can locate gender, race, sexuality, or any of the other ways we divide people up. You won't be able to find the thing that puts you in one category or another, because there's nothing fixed in the world; everything is impermanent, rising and falling, swirling into existence and swirling out again. Again, our views about things are not the things themselves : cultures suggest and enforce stories about gender, but the stories aren't the same thing as fixed gender essences.

Perceiving that she hasn't quite convinced him, the Goddess uses her supernatural powers to change Shariputra into a goddess like herself, while she takes on Shariputra's form. She then asks, "Why don't you transform your female body?"

Shariputra answers, "I don't know how you transformed me into this female body, so I don't know how to transform my way out of it."

The Goddess concludes, "Just as Shariputra isn't female but is manifesting a female body, the buddhas have explained that all phenomena are neither male nor female, nor anything else." As the sutra says earlier about illness, there are causes and conditions that manifest as what we call femaleness or maleness, but there is no feminine or masculine essence for us to identify absolutely with — or to make hugely consequential judgments about, like that you have to be a man to get enlightened.

At this point the Goddess withdraws her supernatural

power and Shariputra returns to his previous form. The Goddess asks him, "Where is your female body now?"

Shariputra says, "My female body doesn't exist, but at the same time it doesn't not exist." There's a turn here : I understand that it's gone ... but there's a way in which it's also still here.

The Goddess says, "All things are like that : not existing, and yet not *not* existing." Now we're getting closer to a contemporary understanding of questions like gender : it matters and it doesn't matter, at the same time, and at different levels. 'It doesn't not exist' is about how it matters. In the material world, gender makes a difference; it has consequence. So it's not that gender isn't true; it's just not necessarily what we think it is, and we're being invited to examine our assumptions about it.

In our practices of sleeping and dreaming,[21] we talk about how a dream body is constellated when we're dreaming, and it's capable of things different from what we're capable of in our waking lives. You can fly, and animals speak to you. That dream body doesn't just come into existence a few hours each night; in some way it's always part of us, even when we're awake. This is what I think the sutra is saying about gender : it both exists and doesn't exist at the same time. How many dream bodies live inside you, as real and as not-real as the dream body you walk through your life in?

---

21 *Practices of the Night*, which are the theme of another handbook in this series

The Room Where Bodhisattvas Are Born

There is no past, present, or future in awakening.
the Goddess

At one point the Goddess says that eight rare things happen in Vimalakirti's room, and we can take 'Vimalakirti's room' to mean the room we enter when we've begun to give birth to ourselves as bodhisattvas. The room is always illuminated with golden light. The light never changes, day or night, and it has nothing to do with the sun and the moon, or electric light for that matter. When we make the bodhisattva vow, the room is radiant all the time, independent of circumstances and conditions. Things don't have to be 'safe' or 'beautiful' for the radiance to be there; it's just inherent to the air. The room is also filled with music that expresses the Way. This music is like the Sermon of the Non-sentient[22] : rocks, grasses, rivers, mountains, the stars, skyscrapers, and suspension bridges are

22   The Sermon of the Non-sentient is related to the Chan teacher Dongshan, who suddenly heard it during an enlightenment experience — though he said you had to hear it with your eyes

expressing the Way all the time, just by their very existence.

When we consider the rain of flowers, the radiance of everything, and the music that's always playing, the Goddess keeps pointing to the beauty of the Way. In the midst of all this daunting philosophy and challenging practice, she reminds us that the Way is beautiful. In the midst of our coming to terms with suffering, pain, unfairness, and difficulty, it's also true that there is great tenderness, courage, kindness, and generosity in the world, and that seems to be the Goddess' particular voice in the room of awakening.

The Goddess continues that those who enter this room are no longer troubled by the kinds of things that tend to trouble us, either the workings of our own heart-minds or the slings and arrows of life. Which doesn't mean that those things don't exist; it means that those in the room aren't troubled by them. We'll return to this in the next section.

All beings come together in this room in a gathering that never ends. The Six Paramitas[23] and other teachings are on some kind of continuous dharma loop, and the same is true for new teachings and deeper commentaries. So there's a grounding in the practices we've come to know so well, and there's always something new happening, too — because we gather together, because we don't think words are bad things, because we speak and listen. The Way is always growing and changing in relationship to circumstances, and everyone in the gathering is participating.

This room has access to the Pure Lands. In our own lives that means that we can always touch the Pure Land inside ourselves, and we can always see the Pure Land that the world is,

---

23   The Six Paramitas or Perfections are the epitome of awakened activity : generosity, decency, forbearance, commitment, meditation, and insight

as Shariputra was suddenly able to at the beginning of the sutra. And, finally, there are inexhaustible storehouses for the benefit of all, containing more than enough to go around. The metaphor of world as storehouse appears frequently in the koans; Dogen said, "The storehouse of treasures opens by itself. You may take them and use them any way you wish."[24] As we spend more time in the room, it becomes more and more apparent that the world is full of treasures, and that we have access to them — as does the thought that we make our lives at the intersection of our bodhichitta and those treasures.

All well and good, Shariputra seems to be thinking, but he still wants to know, "How long will it be until you attain perfect, complete enlightenment?"[25]

The Goddess replies, "I'll never attain perfect, complete enlightenment. Enlightenment doesn't have a fixed location, so you can't attain it." If it doesn't have a fixed location, that means it's everywhere.

Shariputra argues, "The buddhas who are now attaining perfect, complete enlightenment, those who have attained it in the past, and those who will attain it in the future are as numerous as the sands of the Ganges River. What about all of them?" Are you saying that they aren't attaining anything?

The Goddess replies, "It's only with conventional words and numbers that we talk about past, present, and future; there is no past, present, or future in enlightenment."

This conversation is ostensibly about enlightenment in the

---

24   From Dogen's *Fukan Zazengi*, 'Recommending Meditation to Everyone'. Dogen was the 13th-century Zen genius who went to China and brought Chan teachings back to Japan.

25   The Sanskrit term is *annutara samyak sambodhi*

classical sense, which is Shariputra's concern. But we'll borrow the Goddess' supernatural powers and transform enlightenment into awakening, so that it includes endarkenment as well. Then the Goddess is saying that not only is awakening everywhere, it's also timeless. So you can't have missed your chance, nor is awakening something that will happen in the future if you do x, y, and z. It can happen right here, right now; it can only happen right here and now.

One of the healing corollaries to this is that as you awaken, you lose any sense of regret for all that time you wasted, since there's no such thing as wasted time. As awakening flows into the present, it runs not just into the future, but into the past as well. Your past wakes up, too, so there's nothing lost, nothing to regret. All of it is illuminated, and there's no before and after.

Vimalakirti & Manjushri II

Lotuses in the Marsh

If you plant seeds in the sky, they'll never grow.
                                                    Manjushri

The dialogue now returns to Vimalakirti and Manjushri,
picking up some of the points that the Goddess just made
with Shariputra. Manjushri asks how a bodhisattva enters
the way of buddhahood, and Vimalakirti says that it is exactly
in following paths that are, according to various translations,
wrong or unacceptable or simply not-the-way that you find
the buddha path. Vimalakirti then chants one of the sutra's
semi-hypnotic litanies, this one of bad places you might find
yourself in : hell, the land of hungry ghosts, among demons
or private buddhas, and, perhaps surprisingly, nirvana. And
of the afflictive emotions you might feel : anguish, hatred,
anxiety, stupidity, arrogance, greed, aversion, anger, stinginess,
irascibility, laziness, distractedness, deceitfulness, haughtiness,
dissipation. And of challenging conditions — poverty, illness
and disability, humble birth, physical weakness and ugliness,
inarticulateness, old age — and also wealth and abundant

sexual partners. You might even discover that you're a heretic. So many not-the-ways!

And yet ... If you can dis-identify with them in the ways we spoke of earlier, but without holding yourself as superior to and therefore separate from them, you can nurture a peaceful and generous heart — even in the depths of hell, even in the vast emptiness of nirvana. It's probably easy to see why a peaceful and generous heart is an improvement on hell, but it's also more precious than nirvana, because it's how we can extend the healing to others. Problems in the material world need hands and checkbooks and perseverance, which are not possible in the fleshlessness of nirvana. And this peaceful and generous heart is how we extend the healing without exhausting it within ourselves; it is a sustainable state resting on the whole earth, not teetering atop a scaffolding of reaction and fear. Dis-identified but not separate : this is the state of calm attending and wholehearted accompanying that Vimalakirti proposes for bodhisattvas in the process of giving birth to themselves.

Most of the items in this litany of not-the-ways are pretty self-evident, as is the advice embedded with them : share your wealth with others, don't believe what demons tell you. But there's also something deep in the outlier translation of walking 'unacceptable paths.'[26] Unacceptable to whom? Unacceptable in what way? Perhaps this allows us to include not only the self-evident but also those disturbances that are particular — particularly unacceptable — to each of us : those paths that have been ruled off limits by collective expectations, or by our own fears. How does taking those heart-pounding forks in the

---

26   This is John McRae's translation

road bring us closer to the buddha way? It's something like the psychological idea of the shadow, those semi-submerged parts of ourselves that, underneath the trouble they cause, contain huge potential. Jung might have been talking about the awakening power of unacceptable paths when he said that we don't heal our symptoms; our symptoms heal us.

The sutra is repeating that when we try to protect ourselves from the unacceptable not-the-ways, we're also sequestering ourselves from possibilities of awakening. A koan asks, "What is the blown-hair sword?" What is the sword so sharp that if you blew a hair against it, the hair would be cut in two? Earlier, in commenting on the dialogue between the Goddess and Shariputra, we said that the upwelling of anger — or a moment of grief, or the fog of uncertainty — can be the occasion for a profound epiphany. Now Vimalakirti is saying that *anything* can be the blown-hair sword if we're willing to hold ourselves against it; anything along any path can shock us out of habit, out of not seeing, and suddenly the world that a second ago looked either very difficult or very ordinary is radiant as the Pure Land. There are many reasons to exclude nothing from the dream of awakening, and one of them is that anything might be the blown-hair sword.

Vimalakirti then asks Manjushri, "What are the seeds of *tathagata*?"[27] What are the sources of this growing awakening inside us? The first seed is possession of a body; the basic prerequisite for awakening is that you're embodied. Then there's ignorance and partiality (partiality in the sense of choosing some things over

---

27 Tathagata means Thus Come, and it's a title of the Buddha and a quality everything possesses, something like thusness or isness. Tathagata also refers to the awakening inherent in each being, similar to buddha nature.

others); greed, aggression, and denial; the four confusions, the five hindrances, the six senses, the seven consciousnesses, the eight heterodox teachings, the nine sources of anxiety, the ten evil actions — in other words, all the confusions and obstacles and challenges of human psychology and of our lives together.

Our awakening doesn't strike us like a thunderbolt from some otherworldly realm of enlightenment; each of us is born with an inherent radiance, a capacity for awakening known as buddha nature or tathagata, that is inextricable from our bodies and our consciousness, and even from the dumb things we think and do. Manjushri elaborates on this, using a famous image : "It's just like the lotuses, which don't grow on dry upland plains; they grow in the muck and mire of low-lying marshes ... It's only within the mud of the afflictions that sentient beings can give rise to the elements that make up a buddha." He also says, "If you plant seeds in the sky, they'll never grow. Only when you plant them in well-manured soil can they sprout and flourish."

There's a risk in seeing those lotuses as different in nature from the marshes in which they grow; some Buddhist texts talk about lotuses that are pure in spite of the mire beneath them. But let us set aside that *in spite of*. Let us respect the years and the hard-won experiences, the mistakes, revelations, griefs, unexpected graces, regrets, perseverance, and bravery that form our particular marshes, and the lotuses rooted in them. A beautiful image from the koans is of a lotus seen simultaneously above and below the water. Below it's a closed bud floating in the timeless dark; above it's an open flower waving on its stalk in the sun. In the middle is a wide expanse of water and leaves, and a scattering of petals. The lotus of our awakening is all of that at once.

Finally, Manjushri says, if you don't dive into the vast ocean of existence, you'll never find the priceless jewel of awakening. In the heavenly realms where the devas[28] live, everything is perfect and awakening isn't possible because nothing ever changes. It's in *this* world, where our ankles go out from under us, our hearts get broken, and we weep tears that are solvents for whatever is stuck within us, that awakening can happen.

A Chinese poem goes :

You can't light a lamp, there's no oil in the house.
It's a shame to want a light.
I have a way to bless this poverty :
Just feel your way along the wall.

Yingyuan Longqi

Something can happen in the dark that can't in the light of the deva realms, something about simplicity and stillness, vastness and depth — grounded in a world-house of lamps and oil and all the rest. In the velvet dark there's so much less we're compelled to know and do, so much more space for listening. We bless the marvelous poverty of human life by doing what we can only do here, feeling our way along the walls that give texture and shape to the deep nights of our lives. This is what endarkenment means.

---

28   Devas are gods who live in heavens of pleasure and beauty; they aren't immortal, and it's considered auspicious for a deva to be reborn into a human life, in which awakening is possible

Private Buddhas

Other people feel this, too.

Tonglen practice

Vimalakirti continues Manjushri's theme, reiterating that only someone immersed in the world can fully awaken. Private buddhas, who have separated themselves from the world, cannot. That's a startling thing to say : they *cannot* awaken.

"The private buddhas, who have cut off all entanglements, are like people whose faculties are impaired." If you turn away from your relationships, responsibilities, affiliations, dreams, challenges, and everything else that makes up a human life, you wound yourself in fundamental ways. "They can no longer benefit from the teachings; they won't even have the desire to." You become impervious to influence and change, and without yearning there can be no aspiration. In other words, you lose the capacity for bodhichitta. The heart that cares and aspires has been shut down, connections wither, and without them the impulse to seek awakening for the benefit of others dies.

Everyone has run into at least one private buddha in the

meditation hall, remote and severe in demeanor, always having an important reason for not staying after the retreat to help clean up. But whenever we meet semi-mythological figures like the private buddhas in the old texts, we should also consider the ways in which we might carry a bit of them in ourselves.

Perhaps we recognize a tendency to think of awakening as the private pursuit of a personal release from a suffering that also seems private — our own private hell. My suffering is mine alone / my enlightenment is mine alone — two sides of the same illusory coin. Somewhere along the way the private buddhas lose a sense of continuousness between inner and outer lives: we take place in the world, and the world takes place in us. We suffer with the world, and we wake up with the world, too. When you lose the ability to be pierced by the suffering of others, you risk losing the ability to be pierced by their beauty.

In Vimalakirti's room we see that whatever pain we're experiencing is a little shard of the world's suffering that's been given into our care. If we can attend to it and maybe heal it, we're doing that not just for ourselves but for the world. Can you imagine being able to say, about the thing that hurts you most, *If I take care of this, no one else will have to*? That's the power of Tibetan *Tonglen* practice when, as you feel the depths of your own pain, you send out prayers for the healing of everyone else who feels as you do. Instead of your pain isolating you, turning you into a private buddha, it connects you with others and reminds you of our shared humanity. The grand thing about being in Vimalakirti's room is knowing that everyone else in the room is doing the same thing, sharing the demanding and also wondrous work of the world's awakening, sending their energy in your direction as you send yours in theirs.

Roaring Silence

The Sutra that Vimalakirti Speaks is a series of conversations culminating in a roaring silence. It's one of the most famous silences in all of Buddhist literature, and it's still reverberating two thousand years later. Chan's origin story has been described as a history of silences : the first transmission happened when the Buddha twirled a flower and Mahakashyapa smiled;[29] Vimalakirti handed the silence to the world outside the Buddha's garden; and Bodhidharma brought it to China, holding it in a cave for nine years of meditation until it was ripe. Like all myths, this heroic narrative is saying something simple about each of us : we all carry that silence within us. It is the womb in which awakening gestates, where a peaceful

---

29 Mahakashyapa was one of the Buddha's disciples. Once, instead of delivering his usual sermon, the Buddha simply held up a flower, and Mahakashyapa broke into a smile. The Buddha affirmed that in this exchange his heart-mind had been fully transmitted to his disciple.

and generous heart takes form. It is the source of a powerful, non-self-obsessed, courageous energy that flows back into the world as surely as rivers return to the sea.

Vimalakirti asks his guests, "How does a bodhisattva go about entering the gate of nonduality? Each of you, please explain what you understand about that." Many of them step forward and offer first a duality and then a resolution of that duality, usually through a kind of philosophical discourse that's perhaps less interesting to us than it was to them. Here's just a partial list of the dualities they mention :

birth & death
darkness & light
self & other
self & no-self
grasping & rejecting
perception & non-perception
defilement & purity
true & false
form & formless
good & bad
blame & blessing
bondage & liberation
mind & thoughts
eye & objects it observes
ear & sounds
nose & smells
body & tangible things

bodhisattva & private
    buddha aspirations
worldly & unworldly
samsara (world of birth &
    death) & nirvana
exhaustible & inexhaustible
enlightenment & ignorance
correct & erroneous
form & emptiness
real & unreal
four elements (earth, water,
    fire, wind) & space
wisdom & ignorance
created & uncreated
passion & dispassion
mind & phenomena
to yearn for nirvana & to not
    delight in the world

These come in groupings other than two's : buddha, dharma, and sangha are offered as a duality, as are beneficial actions, transgressive actions, and doing nothing. All in all, this section of the sutra reminds us of how much time we spend sorting things into piles and then labeling the piles — according, usually, to our sense of what they mean to us. When the assembly — the many — is done, they turn the question on Manjushri, wielder of the sword that cuts into one : "How does the bodhisattva enter the gate of nonduality?" What's the view of the bright, clear, empty world, as opposed to the complicated world of infinite forms the assembly has just swirled into existence?

Manjushri replies, "As I understand it, to enter the gate of nonduality is to be without words, explanations, meanings, or thoughts, transcending all questions and answers." So Manjushri sweeps everything back into emptiness, saying that you enter the gate of nonduality by not having language, or even thoughts.

There's a bit of irony in Manjushri's *talking about* not thinking or expressing anything, and his preference for emptiness over inquiry is yet another duality, even as we're discussing how to enter the gate of nonduality. It's just so difficult to escape, and that's part of the point.

Then Manjushri turns to Vimalakirti and says, "Each of us has offered an explanation. Now it's your turn to speak. How does the bodhisattva enter the gate of nonduality?"

Vimalakirti remains silent.

Manjushri sighs and says, "Excellent, excellent! Not a word, not even a syllable. This is truly entering the gate of nonduality." (Oh, dear bodhisattvas, can we ever refrain from having an opinion, even about the silence?) Then something happens that foreshadows the koan dialogues of the future : five thousand members of the assembly experience Vimalakirti's silence and immediately enter the gate of nonduality for themselves. In fact, this passage later became a koan,[30] not because it explains something about nonduality but because Vimalakirti's silence is a field which anyone — even someone a thousand years later — might enter and experience for themselves.

Let's have a look at the different kinds of silence in this story. Awhile ago, when the Goddess asked Shariputra how long he's been awakened, he replied, "Liberation can't be spoken of in words, and so I don't know what I can say to you." This is one kind of silence : an inability to speak arising from the idea that it's somehow truer to liberation not to talk. The silence Manjushri just described is of a different sort; it's a negation of thought and expression altogether (although Manjushri's inability to actually remain silent indicates that there's a big gap here between theory and practice).

In contrast to either of these, Vimalakirti's silence is an affirmation. It's not the absence of words but the presence of something else : silence as an expression of the ineffable. That's one of the foundational invitations of the koans : Yes, there's no way to do justice to the ineffable, and as soon as you open your mouth you're in trouble. All true, and please do it anyway. If you can't describe or explain it, so much the better; don't try to. Show it. Become an instance of it. And do it in a way that it becomes visible, apparent, manifest to all of us.

From the koan perspective, that's the deepest kind of conversation we can have. You don't have to make a big

---

30 *Blue Cliff Record* 84

production of it, but it's those moments when we're in each other's presence and we are, with everything we do, expressing the inexpressible, and there's nothing missing and no need to comment on it. In the midst of the heady debate filling his room, Vimalakirti reminds us : this is true, too.

His silence is an invitation into the moment before speech, or the inability to speak, or the rejection of speech. It's as if Vimalakirti is saying that the gate into nonduality isn't in front of you, it's *behind* you, and all you have to do is step back through it. Don't worry about how to step forward yet; pause here, in the silence. Zen expressions like 'no self' and 'no mind' are talking about this moment just before, when the vast empires of self and mind have yet to heave into place, like the cities in the *Game of Thrones* title sequence, and you can see great distances.

The Diamond Sutra, another text introduced to China at about the same time as Vimalakirti's, describes this moment as "abiding nowhere, letting the heart-mind appear." What if you don't think that the first thing you have to do about anything is have a position on it? What if you don't pick and choose ahead of time, leading with the usual from your trusty tool kit? What if, instead, the whole field of you — what you understand and feel, what your body knows, the experiences you've had, your understanding and intuition, your ancestral wisdom, the wisdom radiating off everything in the vicinity — has a chance to appear?

You step back into the moment before, you lean back on abiding nowhere, and then the whole field of you flows into the vast event field that is any moment. The present moment everyone says we should be mindful of stretches from one end of the universe to the other, and from before the beginning of time to after the end of time. That's a lot to be mindful of, so it's lucky that we stretch in all those directions, too. In the space behind the gate of Vimalakirti's thunderous silence, we're taking place with everything. That space is where we touch the vastness, in any ordinary moment of any ordinary day. And the gate also opens *forward* into the event that's about to happen, and we follow the pull of the moment back through the gate.

If all that sounds a little overwhelming — *Gosh, I was just hoping for a cup of coffee* — here's the domestic version, which is exactly the same thing : Mahasattva Fu, another Chinese householder ancestor from roughly the same time, begins a poem with the line, "With empty hands, I pick up the hoe." With empty hands, with hands holding no position or viewpoint, I take the hoe out of the toolshed, lift up the child, type away on the computer. What a relief to feel that we don't have to go through the day manufacturing those vast present moments! We just have to listen for the whisper that rises from silence : *What wants to happen here?* Oh, just a cup of coffee.

And herewith endeth the foolishness of a whole lot of words about Vimalakirti's silence.

The Fragrance of Zen

May it give you as much joy to eat as it gave me to make.

Sujata

After this momentous conclusion to the morning's conversations, Shariputra starts to worry that entering the gate of nonduality is hungry work, and how is everybody going to be fed? Vimalakirti hears his thought and responds by promising the assembly a meal the likes of which they've never yet experienced. (I believe this falls into the category of *Yeah, But What Have You Done for Me Lately?*) He opens a portal to the world on the other side of the galaxy called Many Fragrances that we spoke of earlier, to pick up some miraculous takeout for the bodhisattvas. A single bowl of fragrant rice is brought back, accompanied by nine million Many Fragrances bodhisattvas. Soon 84,000 citizens of Vimalakirti's city, attracted by the food's aroma, also join the assembly, as do a host of various deities. Of course the bowl feeds the assembled millions without being diminished in the slightest.

The bowl of rice is made of mercy, which attracts the

multitudes hungry for it. It's a cosmic force, mercy — and so is the yearning for it. This is one of the moments the text reminds us of why we'd be drawn to take up Vimalakirti's impossible Way : to partake of mercy, to share it with others, and to come to know as deeply as we know anything that it is inexhaustible.

This merciful bowl is reminiscent of the meal that saved Siddhartha's life when he was dying of his austerities. Sujata gave the future buddha the bowl of milk rice she'd prepared for him, saying, "May it give you as much joy to eat as it gave me to make." Sujata's blessing has always seemed to me like the perfect expression of a compassionate life.

These images of enough space in a small room and enough food in a single bowl for multitudes remind us of the mercy of the present moment, which is always enough. And if we hold an awareness of how much we could use a bowl of mercy most minutes of most days, it might make it easier for us to imagine easily passing it around to others, without a whole lot of commentary attached.

Everyone who eats this food begins to exude a wonderful scent, similar to the trees on Many Fragrances. Full up with lunch, full up with the Way, this forest of fragrant beings decides that they'll return to the garden on the outskirts of the city where the Buddha waits. The body of the whole that temporarily divided into two will now be reunited. Vimalakirti hasn't been quite the same since his revelatory silence, and in his new, vast aspect he picks up the entire assembly, along with all their thrones, and carries them on the palm of his hand back to the garden. The world that at the beginning of the story was a problem to be endured or repudiated has become something to carry with us, tenderly, in the palms of our hands.

When they arrive (and Vimalakirti has presumably put

everyone down), Ananda, the Buddha's attendant, says, "You smell really nice! What is that fragrance?" Vimalakirti explains that in our lives there are times when we partake of this bowl of fragrant rice made of mercy, and for awhile we become fragrant ourselves. Ananda asks, "How long does the fragrance last?" Vimalakirti tells him that it's for seven days — meaning for a bit.

We've eaten this merciful meal, and it purifies any poisons within us. This is to say that any afflictions that cause us to cause harm to others are being transformed into the stuff of awakening. Vimalakirti explains that the food will remain un-digested until it's accomplished its work of poison-transforma-tion; the seven days or five lifetimes that it takes us to do that good work is a holy time, and we're fragrant with it. There's an idea that whenever you're doing something ostentatiously, proudly, ornamentally Zen, you have the stink of Zen. I'd like to pair that with the fragrance of Zen, which arises from doing this good work.

After however long it takes, we digest the food and are no longer fragrant with it. As I see it, the scent goes away because the place the work has brought us to has become ordinary; we've made it completely our own. This cycle is repeated throughout our lives : we eat from the bowl of mercy again, we purify again, we become ordinary again, and we move to the next cycle. Each meal provides the fuel to go on to the next thing, and so it goes.

Here's a story about Layman Pang, who was called the Vimalakirti of China. He's visiting a Chan teacher named Daiyu, who's his dharma brother, which means they both had the same teacher, Great Ancestor Ma. They sit down to a lunch together and Layman Pang starts to serve himself from the common bowls.

Daiyu says, "Don't you know that *The Sutra that Vimalakirti Speaks* says that a bodhisattva should never eat anything that's not given?" In other words, you shouldn't be serving yourself, you should only accept food when it's offered to you.

Layman Pang responds, "When I eat, everyone and everything is nourished." And when others eat, I am nourished.

The koans are full of beautiful evocations of this understanding; they liken us to horses and cows, saying that when the horses eat the cows get full. Clouds gather on North Mountain, rain falls on South Mountain. Whatever we're doing, we're doing it within this vast field of interpermeation.

We've come to the close of *The Sutra that Vimalakirti Speaks*, and this image of a fragrant meal from the bowl of mercy lingers as a kind of benediction on whatever you've eaten of these words, whatever you've taken into yourself and are nourished by — your fragrance, the fragrance of an awakening world.

Alternate Coda

The sun revealed in the hands
of an old woman selling fans[31]

Dahui

The Sutra that Vimalakirti Speaks ends with everyone back
in the Buddha's garden, where the assembly is shown another
world called Wonderful Joy, with its splendid adornments,
pure practices, and the impeccable cleanliness of its disciples.
Some of the assembly immediately begin to practice hard, with
the intention of being reborn there, and the Buddha promises
them that they will.

Wait, what?

If you feel pushed to your edges by Vimalakirti's invitation
to love this heartbreaking world, take some comfort in the fact
that the compilers of the sutra apparently did, too. They rush
in at the end to reassure us that, after all, there *is* a ticket out

---

31   This comes from a koan : Someone asked Dahui, "What's it like when
mind and buddha are both forgotten?" Dahui replied, "The sun revealed in
the hands of an old woman selling fans."

of the Tilty World and into a Pure Land in the sky. They're leading us out of the mythic imagination, where the story gets worked out in the kingdom where it takes place, and back into a religious one, where a *deus ex machina* is kind of the whole point. But it's possible to imagine a different ending to the story.

Here's why I believe that matters. In the Introduction, I spoke of the origins of the sutra. We're many generations from those times, and we've seen many cycles of fever, healing, and fever's return. Along the generations we've gathered some powerful medicine, in the form of literature and art, myths and practices, including *The Sutra that Vimalakirti Speaks*. Just now the temperature of the world seems to be rising toward delirium again, reminding us of Vimalakirti's litany of dangerous places. (The realms of the angry gods and hungry ghosts come to mind.) Fortunately we also have the compass and sextant he offers to navigate those places : a peaceful and generous heart, and a space fragrant with awakening where we can meet with our companions to try to be, in Leonard Cohen's immortal words, the balancing monsters of love.

So here's the alternate coda :

A sick bodhisattva, lying on a bed in a room. Perhaps the sick bodhisattva is the world. The world with its broken-open heart, its miseries and its portals to wondrous places across the cosmos. The world with its strange wisdom and air thick with compassion. The world filled to overflowing with beings of all kinds. The world of lamentation. The world of song.

To meet Vimalakirti is to meet the world. It is to open your heart to the heart of the world, to see that your heart is the world's heart, the world's heart is yours. Tender and wrenching, that heart : so devastating when it constricts into stone or beats the rhythm of war, and so very poignant in its hopeful perseverance, from spring's new grass to a gathering of students in a refugee camp.

To meet Vimalakirti is to meet the sick bodhisattva within you. Sick : in pain, struggling, weary — and also humble, yearning, pulled by underworld currents toward something essential. Bodhisattva : already radiant with a love bigger than pain. Lying on a bed : held up by the earth, resting on the vast night of space.

To meet Vimalakirti is to begin to heal, discovering your own absolute, unquestioned, unmitigated, unbuffered, uncompromised allegiance to the life you actually have. You can save your own life, with its lush gardens and sickbeds and bowls of mercy, and you can help in your infinitesimal and essential way to save the life of all the other creatures in gardens and hospital wards. Sometimes it's so very hard, but you will have the help of others, and, once in awhile, a soft rain of blossoms from a passing Goddess.

About the Author

Joan Sutherland is a teacher in the Zen koan tradition, which she is re-imagining with allegiance to the root spirit of the koans and to their profound potential for vivifying, subverting, and sanctifying our lives. In her unique vision, awakening is as much about endarkenment as enlightenment. In 2014 she retired from working directly with students to focus on writing. She now lives on the coast of northern California.

About Cloud Dragon

Cloud Dragon : The Joan Sutherland Dharma Works makes her groundbreaking teachings widely available, and is the place to access her work in written, audio, and video forms. Subscribers receive talks and other material from the archives every month. We're a nonprofit that relies on your tax-deductible contributions.

Publications and Resources from Cloud Dragon

Acequias & Gates
Miscellaneous Koans and Miscellaneous Writings on Koans
A book containing the Pacific Zen School's koan collection,
Joan Sutherland's writings on our unique style of koan practice,
with Ciel Bergman's paintings

The Radiance of the Dark
A short video on how awakening is as much about
endarkenment as enlightenment

Small Dreams
Six short videos on our tradition

Radiance of the Dark Podcast
Free and available on iTunes

Pilgrim's Bundle
Handbooks on traditional philosophy, practices,
and poetry in a contemporary voice

For these and other resources, please visit
joansutherlanddharmaworks.org

Made in the USA
Charleston, SC
13 November 2016